the Wanderer for WonderWhat

Rob Woodrum

RobWoodrum.com • WonderWhat.net

The Wanderer for Wonderwhat
Copyright ©2006, 2016 by Rob Woodrum
All rights reserved.
No part of this book may be reproduced or transmitted in any form or by any means without permission by the author, except in the case of brief quotations embodied in critical articles or reviews.

Illustrated by Rob Woodrum
Edited by Bradley Woodrum
Art Direction by Jessica Bunnell

Published 2006, 2016
Printed by Createspace in the United States of America
ISBN-10: 1508624240 - ISBN-13: 9781508624240

DEDICATION

It is with the greatest of love, affection and wonder that I dedicate this book to my loving wife and co-conspirator Robbie. Our long walks and conversations were the embryogenesis of our adventure in searching for church. She is my lover-friend and sounding board, whose input and opinion has provided the shape of this work.

Jessica, Daniel, Bradley and Janelle, how could I ever express how important you have been in shaping me into a man. We all had to grow up together and now as adults who share in this ministry, your input, advice and leadership continue to inspire me. Thank you, I love you.

I also dedicate this book to my extended family of Eastgate. I am convinced that I am the most blessed man on earth to have such wonderful friends and such a great community to hang out with. God bless you, you children of God!

ONE

The Wanderer was racing down the hallway outside of the "Big Room", the affectionate name given to the church's sanctuary. He was trying to get to his office for one last glance at his notes before he stood up to teach. As he rounded the corner, he almost walked right into a woman he didn't recognize who was standing halfway into the hallway. He moved to the left of her making as graceful a dodge as he could and realized that she wasn't the only one there. The woman was actually at the end of a line of women who were waiting to get into the restroom.

There's a line for the bathroom? the Wanderer thought to himself.

Then he noticed there was a line of two men waiting for the men's room.

A momentary surge of panic swept over the Wanderer and he retraced his steps back down the hallway, ducking into the empty media room. He stood in the darkness, amid the glow of computer screens and looked through the two-way glass at the Big Room.

Where did all these people come from? the Wanderer thought. How do we take care of all these people? Who's in charge of this?

The Wanderer left the dark room and again moved down the hallway toward the coffee house and out toward an adjoining wing of offices in the old strip mall where the church was located.

I have an office. It's expected that I have an office.

His brother, five years his senior, was sitting in the chair to the side of the Wanderer's desk.

"Mind if I sit in here for a moment?" asked his brother.

"Not at all," said the Wanderer as he eased himself into his chair behind his desk.

I have a desk.

"Lotta' people here today," said his brother, watching through the office window as people were filing in through the main entrance of the building. "They just keep coming in too."

"First service was crowded, and from the looks of it, the second one will be full, too," said the Wanderer, also watching the people walk across the broad courtyard that led to the entrance. It was late afternoon and the Florida sun was fully flexing its might, enveloping everything and everyone with a shimmering heat. Everyone he saw was dressed in cool and comfortable clothing, refusing to let the heat dissuade them from gathering together.

"How'd this happen?" he asked, squinting his eyes.

"Not sure, but I do know it's all your fault. It was your idea to start a church," said his brother. Then, mimicking a whiny voice he said, "I hate church; let's start a different kind of church; it'll be fun!"

They both laughed.

"I didn't think it would get like this. This isn't the way I had imagined it" the Wanderer shrugged.

"Doesn't everyone know that we don't know what we're doing?"

"But see, maybe that means something. Maybe it shows that it's not about us, right? I mean, if it were, it would be a debacle. This has a life that has nothing to do with who we are. This is exactly what we were hoping for, something that had no religious agenda, a place where anyone is accepted. No hang-ups on church subculture stuff, just real people loving Jesus. It's really happening and there seems to really be a need beyond my own personal angst. It must be something God's doing, because two screw-ups like us couldn't have done this." The Wanderer started feeling better as he listened to his own words.

It was true; this community had not formed by some marketing design. People were coming from all directions, drawn to the same simplicity that had drawn the Wanderer to begin with. They came from High-Church backgrounds to no church backgrounds. They came young, old and middle aged. They were well dressed and dressed down. Tattoos and piercings mingled right in with gray hair and ties. Republicans sat next to Democrats. Military vets warmly embraced hipsters.

All of them were unique, but all of them were hungry for something real.

How did we get here? How did this happen? the Wanderer thought, watching from across the courtyard as some leather clad bikers held the entrance door open for an elderly couple.

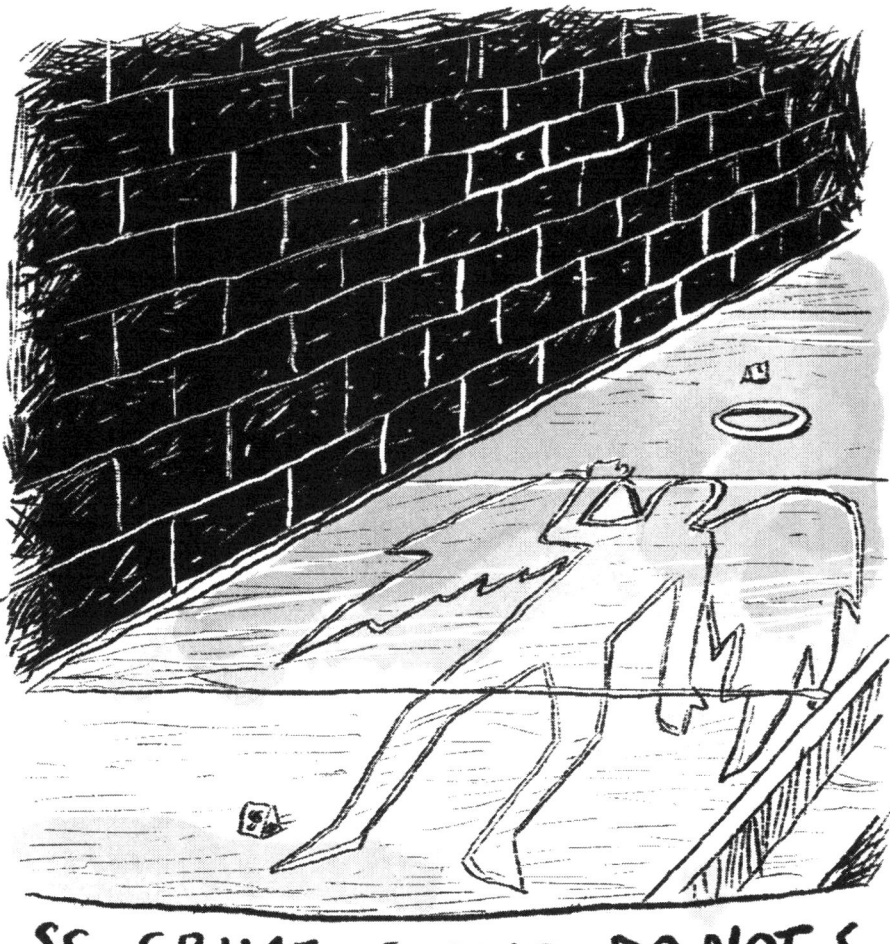

TWO

"All I'm saying is I don't think I can go along with some of our church doctrines in good conscience." The Wanderer stood facing the Preacher who leaned on his pulpit and looked away from him as he surveyed his congregates engaged in after-service conversations. The Wanderer had patiently waited his turn to mount the intimidating platform and approach the Preacher. Seven steps up. The Wanderer had counted them while he waited nervously in line. Seven is the number of perfection in the Bible, he thought, and wondered if it had been intentionally designed.

"Go along?" the Preacher turned and faced the Wanderer. He repeated the words back to him as though he had caught him in a crime. "Go along with God's Word? Go along with Truth? What do you mean?"

A cold sickness spread across The Wanderer's stomach; he could see where this was going. The tenor of the Preacher's voice had changed; his smile had receded back into a thin line on his face. Truth and God's Word were the leverage points the Preacher used to shift his weight against the Wanderer, like a boxer edging his opponent towards the ropes.

I want Truth, he thought, I love God's Word.

Already, he could feel the struggle, feel the pressure to conform. He had the sensation of leaning backwards even though he knew he was standing upright. He looked at the Preacher's face and saw in his eyes that familiar look of superiority, that look of an elevated man who considered himself the right hand of God, whose arguments were flawless because the Spirit inspired them.

Right then, the Wanderer woke up.

He had been struggling to awaken for months, maybe years. He had heard unfamiliar voices and strained to focus on peripheral shadows through bleary eyes. Slogging through an opaque dreamscape of religious obligation he had seen flashes of light, like sunshine piercing gaps in a forest. Suddenly, as though someone were slapping him to bring him into consciousness, he found a new clarity.

"No," he said, "this isn't a question of God's Word or His truth. What I question is your truth and what you are calling God's Word. I'm not so sure you're right and I just don't think I can keep going in the direction this church is going. Not in good conscience, at least." The Wanderer could barely believe what he'd just heard himself say. There was a thrill in the pit of his stomach and he struggled with all his will to stop his hands from shaking or his eyes from watering.

The Preacher spoke through his teeth: "Well what have you been doing here all these years if you haven't been hearing from God? It just shows how stupid you are for sitting under my teaching for so long if you don't believe it's God's Word?

Sitting under your teaching, the Wanderer thought. That's a good description, isn't it? He could feel the aching in his bones from the crushing weight of sitting under this man's teaching. He was weary from it.

"You're so right," said the Wanderer, never leaving the Preacher's eyes. "That does make me rather stupid. The good news is I can still learn."

The Wanderer descended the seven stairs of the platform and met his wife and children in the foyer. He pressed the door open for his family as they walked outside. The air was warm, a stark difference from the cool of the air-conditioned atmosphere of the building they were exiting. They said nothing as they walked. His wife could tell from his clenching jaw just how the talk had gone. She herded their four children through the parked cars toward the old blue station wagon that had hauled them faithfully to this place for years.

The Wanderer turned back towards the church building and swept his eyes over its provincial, log-cabin inspired architecture. The simple lines and angles were so familiar that he could trace them in his sleep. It was only a building but it had always seemed to be so much more. It had conveyed a personality and within those walls his very identity had been sculpted. He had loved that building and all that it stood for in his thinking.

As if looking at it for the first time he could see that it was merely a building.

He knew he would never come back again.

THREE

In a much bigger, paved parking lot, the Wanderer and his family sat in their old blue station wagon as he screwed up his courage to "try" yet another church. The Wanderer surveyed the building they were preparing to enter while his wife worked furiously to keep a cowlick from standing at attention on her son's scalp.

The building was large with a great wall of glass windows that faced the parking lot. Two rows of flags from around the world lined the walkway toward the entrance where well-dressed families were already entering. The place exuded an official air and reminded the Wanderer of the U.N. Building. The rippling flags reminded him that he was a foreigner encountering new customs and unknown expectations. His stomach began to churn.

They unloaded from their station wagon and the children marched in line between the two parents as they stepped into the human stream that led into the interior of this latest attempt to find their place in the church.

Just inside, the customary greeters stood on either side of the four sets of double doors. Each person entering was greeted with a smile and a bulletin was pressed into his or her hands. The perfumed, antiseptic smell of church wafted up to greet the Wanderer's nostrils. He wondered about that -- why every church had the same smell. Did it come in a can? Odor de' church?

"Good to see you again," said the smiling greeter. She was a woman past middle age who clearly had no intention of admitting so. Her hair was big, according to the style of the day; her make-up was excessive, and her dark pantsuit fit snugly on her well kempt physique. She wore a plastic name tag that had the church's logo on it, and the word "connections" underneath.

She extended a bulletin toward the Wanderer with a thin hand which was crisscrossed with veins and bracelets and rings.

"This is our first time here," said the Wanderer.

"Oh!" exclaimed the woman. "Well, welcome to our church!"

She reached behind her to a stack of burgundy folders that sat on a small table. On the cover, in gold letters, was the word "welcome" and underneath the name of the church and the logo.

"You'll find out all you need to know in our visitor's packet. God bless you!" she said and turned, with bulletin in hand, to the next entering person.

As the Wanderer's wife shuffled their children through the honeycombed children's wing, he sat down in a pew with the visitor's packet. He could feel the weight of unspoken requirements pressing against his inner frame again. It was a familiar feeling and he couldn't be sure if it was actually imposed on him or if it was an outgrowth of his own expectations and requirements. No matter it's source, the resulting feeling was that of dread.

He opened the folder like a man about to read his sentencing in court.

Each pocket of the folder brimmed with forms, tri-fold brochures and gifts. A pen with the church's logo on it. A cassette tape labeled "A special word for you from our Pastor." Forms to fill out for contact information. Envelopes to place a one-time offering in and a separate one for an ongoing pledge.

The amount of effort and money that had gone into the packet was impressive, yet intimidating. He felt as though he were being pressured to buy something, as though this were all part of a carefully crafted sales pitch. His stomach twisted.

The Wanderer studied all the contents carefully, even after he had assessed it all sufficiently. He kept his head bowed, intently absorbing the information from the packet, hoping to avoid eye contact with someone who would see that he was all alone.

God is present with His church, the Wanderer thought. The Body of Christ has many and varied expressions.

It was his mantra, his rote explanation as to why he was here: Somehow, God moves here, speaks here, reveals Himself here, and I am here to find Him.

The lights went dim in the auditorium and the Wanderer's wife just made it to their pew as the first rhythmic blasts started from the band. From down the three main aisles that led toward the elevated platform at the front of the sanctuary, a parade of women walked with brightly colored banners which flowed gracefully behind them declaring, among other things, that Jesus was Lord.

Stage lights came on abruptly, highlighting a large shouldered man in a black suit with long, curly and heavily gelled hair. He stepped out to the front of the stage with a wireless microphone and shouted, "Let everything that has breath praise the Lord!" at which time the large gathering of people became a cacophony of shouts and clapping.

You are real, I do believe that, the Wanderer prayed, silently. I know You had something in mind when You instituted the church. There has to be a reason for it. You said you would be with us – but where are You here? I can't feel You, I can't see You, and with all this noise I can't hear a thing. I know You must be here, but where? What is the purpose of this?"

FOUR

The Wanderer and his family had drifted from church to church. They experienced high church traditions and small Pentecostal outposts. Once again, they found themselves in a new and peculiar formation of Christianity. The Wanderer had dubbed it the "Jewish Wannabe" church because of the Eastern influenced music all sung in minor keys and the use of the name "Yeshua" in place of "Jesus."

He had tried several times to open up with people, looking for someone who could relate to his plight, anxious to find a kindred soul who could understand.

The Wanderer had confided in a man, "I love Jesus, I really do, but I just can't seem to get a handle on church. I've been in church all my life; my father was a minister. I believe there should be a church, but for some reason I just can't seem to come to grips with our current expression of it."

The soft-spoken man looked at him for a long time. His glasses looked like concentric outlines of the dark rings around his eyes. His hair was balding and gray, and he wore a bushy, gray mustache. He exhaled a long and almost exaggerated sigh, stared thoughtfully at the floor and said, "Maybe you've set your standards too high. Maybe you need to accept that there is no perfect church. I don't like everything I see in church but that doesn't matter to me. I'm here to support my pastor. I'm part of this church and I want to make sure that its services run smoothly and God is glorified. Maybe you should just grit your teeth and dive in, like you would into a cold swimming pool. It will be hard at first, but soon, you'll become acclimated to the temperature and you'll be just fine."

He looked at the Wanderer hopefully.

With each soft-spoken word, the Wanderer could feel energy being drained from himself like a flower being hung upside down to dry. The man didn't understand the Wanderer's plight and it was clear that he really had no intention of questioning anything. The man had admitted freely that he was there to support, what? Not people, no, to support a pastor and a church service.

"If I stay here," the Wanderer said with every shred of earnestness he could muster, "I don't know if I'll survive it, internally."

"You're overreacting."

"No, no really. And I don't mean here, as in this church. I mean here in church, church as we know it. I'm groping around looking for something real and all I come up with are slogans and sentimental arguments about a perfect church and those things are nowhere near what I'm talking about."

He paused and studied the man's expressionless face. The Wanderer plunged ahead.

"I'm trying to find the connecting point between real life and church. I believe God is real and I believe the church is really supposed to be here, but for what? What is the church? Is it designed to accomplish anything? Is it working? Where does my Sunday morning intersect with my Monday afternoon? How much of my life becomes a part of the church? How much is my own?" The Wanderer realized his voice had risen in pitch.

"Maybe you're thinking too much about it." said the man, bringing the conversation to a close.

There were several more Sundays of visiting new churches where the Wanderer had shaken hands with aggressively friendly ministers, filled out forms and heard absolute assurances that God would show him that this church was the place for him. The Wanderer felt like a rubber band stretched to its limit, trembling under pressures that began to exceed the edge of flexibility.

"I'm done." He told his wife. "I can't keep visiting churches. I'm going to stay home this Sunday."

"What about the kids? Do they quit going to church too? Are we okay with them learning about God from classmates and TV?"

The Wanderer turned away from his wife. He had no real answer. He didn't like the sound of what she was saying, but it was the inevitable conclusion if he were to stick to his decision. He was trapped again, painted into the corner where religion and exhaustion meet.

"I don't know. I mean, that's not what I really want, I just–" his voice trailed off. "I'm just saying I can't go to church for now. It's not a forever thing, I just have to figure out where I am on this."

"Well, I'm going. I'm going to make sure our kids have some peer interaction with a Christian influence and that can't happen if we just stay home. I'll go just for Wednesday services at the last place we went. You don't have to come."

The Wanderer ached at her words. This was real pain. He didn't want to leave his wife to fend for their children's spiritual well-being but he was weak. He had no strength to go on. His bones couldn't bear the weight of just attending meetings and pretending that was enough. There had to be answers, but they were so hard to find.

If I were smarter, he thought, if I just knew how to phrase my questions. But I'm not and I can't. So I'll wait.

FIVE

The Wanderer stood in a cavernous room with arched ceilings like an old Roman cathedral. Shafts of light angled down from high, narrow windows that tapered to a point.

In the center of the room, a group of men filled what appeared to be a huge bag with hot air from a bellows near a fire. The bag was a patchwork of materials sewn together with thick rope stitches. The bag began to undulate and fill out. It bobbed on the ground and danced upward.

"They're trying to make it float. They've worked really hard at it," said a voice from behind the Wanderer. He turned, but saw only a fleeting blur of a human form in his peripheral vision, like a tear in the corner of his eye, blinked away when he tried to see it.

"They'll have to build something that will keep it off the ground because it just can't float on its own," said the voice.

The Wanderer watched in amazement as men like insects crawled all over the bag, erecting scaffolds and connecting ropes to pulleys. They worked at an exaggeratedly quick pace, and before long, an enormous mechanical construction emerged in the cavernous room, all but hiding the original bag. It was a thing of wonder. Wood, metal, and even parts that seemed organic. There were smokestacks that chugged out an oily smoke and the whole contraption made a low rhythmic thrum. There were propellers on the sides and near the top, all whirring at an alarming rate but making no wind at all. Wires and cables and ropes were wound around the thing forming an impenetrable web. All across the construction men were moving on catwalks and platforms, turning dials, stoking fires, and pulling ropes. There was the regular clang of hammers echoing through the great room. The acrid smell of machine oil mixed with the pungent stink of human perspiration. All the people near this odd formation were occupied with some sort of activity. Everyone was sweating and all had an aura of weariness about them.

Here it is, thought The Wanderer. My frustration has a shape to it.

The people working on the machine reminded him of the factory workers from some old dystopian movie. As he watched them, he felt a strange sense of indignation rising. He hated this thing without even knowing for sure what it was. He found himself desperately wanting it torn down and abandoned. He wanted the people to quit slaving over this monster.
He wanted for them what he wanted so desperately for himself: Rest.

"This is the machine. It's been around for a long, long time. Do you think it's your job to tear it down?" asked the voice.

"I can try," said the Wanderer, walking toward the machine, rolling up his sleeves.

"STOP!"

The Wanderer stood still, not taking his eyes off the machine. "That's not for you to do. Don't go anywhere near the outside edges or you'll be torn to pieces." The voice came nearer, right up behind him, almost whispering in his ear. The Wanderer was afraid to look back but listened intently.

"Do you see that opening?" Right near the floor, in the center of the maze of wires, ropes and cables, sat an opening just large enough for a man to fit through.

The hair on the back of the Wanderer's neck began to stand on end.

"Go in there." The voice was closer now and the Wanderer could almost feel a warm breath on his neck. "Go deep inside. Forget what's out here."

The clang and chug of the machine echoed off the walls of the great hall. The Wanderer stood frozen in place, still faintly sensing the breath from the voice behind him.

"You'll find your answer at the heart."

The Wanderer's eyes fluttered open. He was in his bedroom, staring up at the ceiling fan.

The details of the dream were acute and penetrating his half-wakened stupor. As the images replayed in his mind a smile began spreading across his face.

SIX

He refilled his wife's cup of coffee, spilling some onto the table. There was an excited spring in his step. For the Wanderer it was the proverbial moment of clarity. He knew that a person should never go off on a life-quest based on a dream because there are many different fuels for dreams. Yet this was different somehow and he knew he could never explain it.

"What we'll do is take everything we know about church, and I do mean everything, and throw it on the floor. We'll start from scratch as though we'd never heard of church to begin with. We'll just let Jesus pick out the pieces He intended to be part of His church!" the Wanderer exclaimed to his wife.

"Sounds great," said the Wanderer's wife as she buttered a piece of toast, "but you're using a lot of metaphor. What does it mean in real life?"

"I guess what I mean is: Concerning everything we associate with church; we'll press the question 'why?' on it."

"Why?"

"Exactly!"

"No, I mean why are we doing this?" She said, her head slightly tilted to the side.

"Ok, let's try this. When I say 'church,' what are the first things that come to your mind?" the Wanderer asked.

"Hmm, well I guess the church should be about–"

The Wanderer cut her off, "No, no, no! Don't give me the answers you think are right concerning church. This is more like word association. When you hear the word 'church,' tell me just what pops into your mind, what images are conjured up?"

"Alright," she said, closing her eyes. "A white building with a steeple, pews, offerings, dressing up and trying to get spots out of the kid's shirts on the run!" she laughed.

"Ok then! Let's start with that. Why a white building with a steeple? Is that something in the Bible or did that just come as a tradition over time? In fact, why do we automatically associate a building with church? If someone asks where a church is located, we instinctively give driving directions to a building. We never think of a bunch of people. Why?" He was talking with his whole body, and he could feel the fire in his belly.

The Wanderer's wife smiled, got up from the table and started clearing the breakfast dishes. "It appears we're on the verge of a new mania."

"So from zis moment, I no longer am familiar wit zis…how you say, church?" he said with an exaggerated French accent.

"How you say, help with zee dishes?"

"I'll have to go back to the beginning. Start with the Bible; see everything that pertains to any kind of description of the church, its government, its structure and format. See what's really there and what isn't," he said, watching a squirrel through the kitchen window as it was frantically digging in the yard.

"Sounds like a lot of work." said his wife as she turned on the kitchen faucet.

"Sounds like a lot of fun!"

For the Wanderer, the horizons had broken wide open. There was no turning back.

SEVEN

The Wanderer took his Bible and shook it with the pages down as though trying to shake something out of it. With a flip of his wrist he tossed it on the table where he was sitting. His journey into Scripture had begun with such high hopes. In his mind he had imagined coming across whole passages that had been ignored or forgotten, like an ancient treasure trove which held the keys to unlocking the mystery of what the church is supposed to be.

His first endeavor had been a huge disappointment. Pastors, so far in his journey, had been central to the identification of the church, so it made sense to start with them. He'd find out what they were supposed to be doing and why they were really there.

To his chagrin, he found them mentioned in only a few verses and there just in passing. That wasn't the only information lacking. There were no descriptions of meetings apart from Paul's corrections to the Corinthians, and even there, what was said was so foreign, he couldn't connect it to a practical concept. There were no ministry descriptions at all, just lists of ministry types with no practical information about how they were to operate. There was no indicator as to when the church should meet. No mention of children's needs. No order of authority. Could an apostle trump a bishop? The book was silent.

"This is absurd!" the Wanderer said to his Bible. "I mean, the whole thing about Christianity is establishing the church on earth, and you don't even describe what it looks like? The focal point for Christians around the world is the church and you can't devote even one chapter to a start-up guide or creating a checklist for the mandatory ingredients! That's just stupid!"

The Bible did not respond.

This was an impossible task. He couldn't pretend that he'd never heard of church and go strictly to the Bible to find out what it is. The Bible provided the doctrines and the premise, but not a description of the thing itself. It was like trying to see a landscape in a Jackson Pollock painting.

This was bad news for his plan. There was no way to arrive at the concept of church without a historical reference point to start from. The church as he'd known it had its origin in the doctrines and premises of the Bible but was now the product of its own history. There was no way of conceiving the church apart from its story up to now.

He realized that he would have to approach this from a different tack. Instead of pretending he'd never heard of church and discovering what it looked like from the Bible, he would have to go the other way around. He would have to disassemble every aspect of church as he had known it and drag it all, piece by piece, to the Bible and see if it had merit, see if it was based on the original intent and premise of the church.

His wife's warning that it sounded like a lot of work came back to him. He sighed, looked at his Bible and asked, "So where do I begin?"

EIGHT

Sitting on the edge of a marina dock, the Wanderer tried to write. It was hard going. Attempting to compress thoughts into manageable pieces that could be expressed intelligibly was a lot of work. Especially when he wasn't even sure what it was he was trying to say. He filled pages with statements and questions:

In my search, I'm finding very little in church as we know it that is relevant to my everyday life and culture. Shouldn't the church be able to exist in any culture or generation and adapt to address the felt needs?

Church subculture - language, dress, worldview. The idea comes across that if the world wants help, they have to have their needs prescribed to them and conform to the subculture. Where do we cross the line into dishonesty? Why do we never seem to be real people when we're in the pews? Why do I feel immediate pressure to meet unspoken expectations in any expression of the church I've encountered?

Where does a creed end and groupthink begin?

All these random thoughts were yielding no answers, and his fear that he would turn into a bitter, anti-church agitator was growing more and more real.

The Wanderer walked from the marina down to the library. He meandered through different sections until landing in the magazine room. He sat down in a well-worn yellow chair that bore the design tastes of the sixties. His eyes scanned the magazines on the old, wooden shelf.

The cover of a Christian History magazine was emblazoned in bold type: "Worship in the Early Church."

Like metal seized by a magnet, he got up and took the magazine back to his chair. He read it from cover to cover. Reaching into his pocket to retrieve his notebook he went back through the magazine and wrote down the names and titles that had been quoted in various articles.

He copied word for word an excerpt that had been highlighted from Justin Martyr's writings. It read:

… And on the day called Sunday, all who live in cities or in the country gather together to one place and the memoirs of the apostles or the writings of the prophets are read, as long as time permits; then, when the reader has ceased, the president verbally instructs and exhorts to the imitation of these good things. Then we all rise together and pray, and, as we before said, when our prayer is ended, bread and wine and water are brought and the president in like manner offers prayers and thanksgivings, according to his ability, and the people assent, saying Amen; and there is a distribution to each and a participation of that over which thanks have been given and to those who are absent a portion is sent by the deacons. And they who are well to do, and willing, give what each thinks fit; and what is collected is deposited with the president, who provides for the orphans and widows and those who, through sickness or any other cause, are in want and those who are in bonds and the strangers staying among us; and in a word, is the protector of all who are in need.

But Sunday is the day on which we all hold our common assembly because it is the first day on which God, having wrought a change in the darkness and matter, made the world; and Jesus Christ our Savior on the same day rose from the dead. For He was crucified on the day before that of Saturn (Saturday); and on the day after that of Saturn, which is the day of the Sun, having appeared to His apostles and disciples, He taught them these things which we have submitted to you also for your consideration.

The Wanderer read and re-read the excerpt. By the fourth time through tears began to flow. Not just a trickle down his cheek but a gushing torrent of emotion.

He looked up through bleary eyes to see an older gentleman watching him.

The Wanderer tried his best to salvage a little dignity, wiping his face with the back of his hand and sniffing back the wetness from his nose.

The man was still watching him, a look of concern building on his brow.

The Wanderer looked back at him and realized he needed to offer some sort of explanation. He held up the magazine, shrugged, pleaded with his face and said, "It's just so simple."

Again, the urge to weep swept over him and he knew he had to leave.

The Wanderer spent the next few months buried in books. He read the Shepherd of Hermes; he read all of Justin Martyr's 1st and 2nd apologies. He read The Octavius of Minucius Felix, Polycarp and Ignatius and so many others. Yet it was the discovery of the Didache that stirred him again, the way he had been stirred at the library.

It was simplicity that drew him in. He began to feel he was nearing the heart.

NINE

"Start a homegroup? You mean just start a Bible study out of nowhere? Who would be coming to it?" the Wanderer's wife asked.

"I don't know yet. That's the crazy part of it, isn't it?"

"But, I guess if God's in this, those kinds of details would work themselves out," she said, careful not to deflate his excitement.

"Well, yeah, they would."

"This is exciting!" said the Wanderer's wife.

Her response was perplexing to the Wanderer. He thought for sure he'd have to explain himself more than this. Did she really get what he was proposing? He had imagined that she'd call him crazy, a dreamer.

"I'm talking about, you know, starting what would essentially be our version of church."

She smiled at him. "I think I'm able to grasp the concept, dear. You've been talking about this incessantly for months on end. Of course I understand and I'm with you." She kissed him on the cheek.

It had been amazingly simple to convince his wife, brother and sister-in-law to go out on this limb. He couldn't deny that there was a "rightness" to it all. His fear of becoming an embittered objector to church had only one solution. You can either sit around and complain about how things are, or you can offer yourself as an instrument of change, he thought.

And now the change was coming.

Months later the Wanderer ran excitedly into the living room where his wife was.

"Can I read something to you?" he asked her.

"Sure, what is it?" she said, tying a bow knot on their son's shoe.

"Remember how Luther nailed the 95 Theses to the church door in Wittenberg?"

"Yes?"

"Well, I have my own, I don't know, thesis, manifesto, whatever!"

"Whatcha' going to nail it to?"

"I was thinking of nailing it to a window somewhere since a door's already been done. Are you going to listen to this or not?"

"Go ahead," she said, laughing.

"It's called: 'Why I Hate Church.'"

"Hmmm, don't beat around the bush so much. Tell us what you really think," she said, still laughing.

"Come on, I'm serious here," he said, laughing with her.

"Ok, I'm ready now, let's hear it."

WHY I HATE CHURCH

*Ever wonder **why** you come to church?*

Ever wonder where the choir arrangements are described in the Bible?

Ever wonder why God wants you to sit in unspeakable boredom as you endure irrelevant rituals in order to please Him?

Ever wonder where the passage on the dress code for Sunday mornings is in the Bible?

Ever wonder what makes the "pulpit" holy or the front of the church building "holy ground?"

*Ever wonder why Christianity seems like a spectator sport? Ever wonder if this thing could carry on nicely without **you**?*

*Ever notice that for the most part, it carries on nicely without **Jesus**?*

We can trace our problems all the way back to our initial definition of the term. We speak the language of "church." But what is church? These are the things we begin with:

> 1) The word "church," as such, is not found in the New Testament anywhere. The word "church" comes from the root word "kuriakon" in the Greek, transliterated to "circe" in old English. The word kuriakon means "a building set aside for the Lord's use." The word church, which comes from the word kuriakon has come to encompass all the various aspects of the common assembly, yet it has no Scriptural support and is usually still referring to a building which has a depersonalizing effect.

> 2) The word "ekklesia" is the term used in Scripture to describe the common assembly. It is derived from "ek" (out) and "kaleo" (to call). It is a common Greek term to describe people called out from their homes to a gathering place for the discussion of public business…

The manifesto went on and on, using verbose language to sound important and labored over obvious conclusions. No matter, the Wanderer loved it. For the first time he had a sense of clarity about what he was looking for and where he was now headed. For him it was a storyboard that he could work from; a rise on the landscape from which he could view the surrounding terrain.

This was the ideal. It was simple and he kept reducing it down, peeling things back to the rudimentary elements. Church was supposed to be a hangout. A club, so to speak. An exclusively focused club that anyone could visit or join. Church was supposed to be a place where people who wanted to follow Jesus could hang out together. And what were they supposed to do while they hang out together? Support and encourage each other. Become equipped to live out Jesus through their daily lives in the larger world.

That was it.

Since the Bible didn't describe a church meeting, then anything that worked toward the basic goals of hanging out, loving Jesus, caring for each other and demonstrating Jesus could be included in a meeting. On the other hand, anything that didn't work toward those goals could be jettisoned without hesitation. There was no mandate to do things because they had traditionally been done. Real needs would find real solutions. If there were no needs being met by any given activity of the church, they would abandon it without regret.

This was the ideal. The big question on the Wanderer's mind was: Would it work? Could it stay simple? Was the juggernaut of the 21st Century Evangelical American church too powerful for anyone to resist moving in its flow?

The Wanderer thought about his dream of the machine. "Time will tell," he thought.

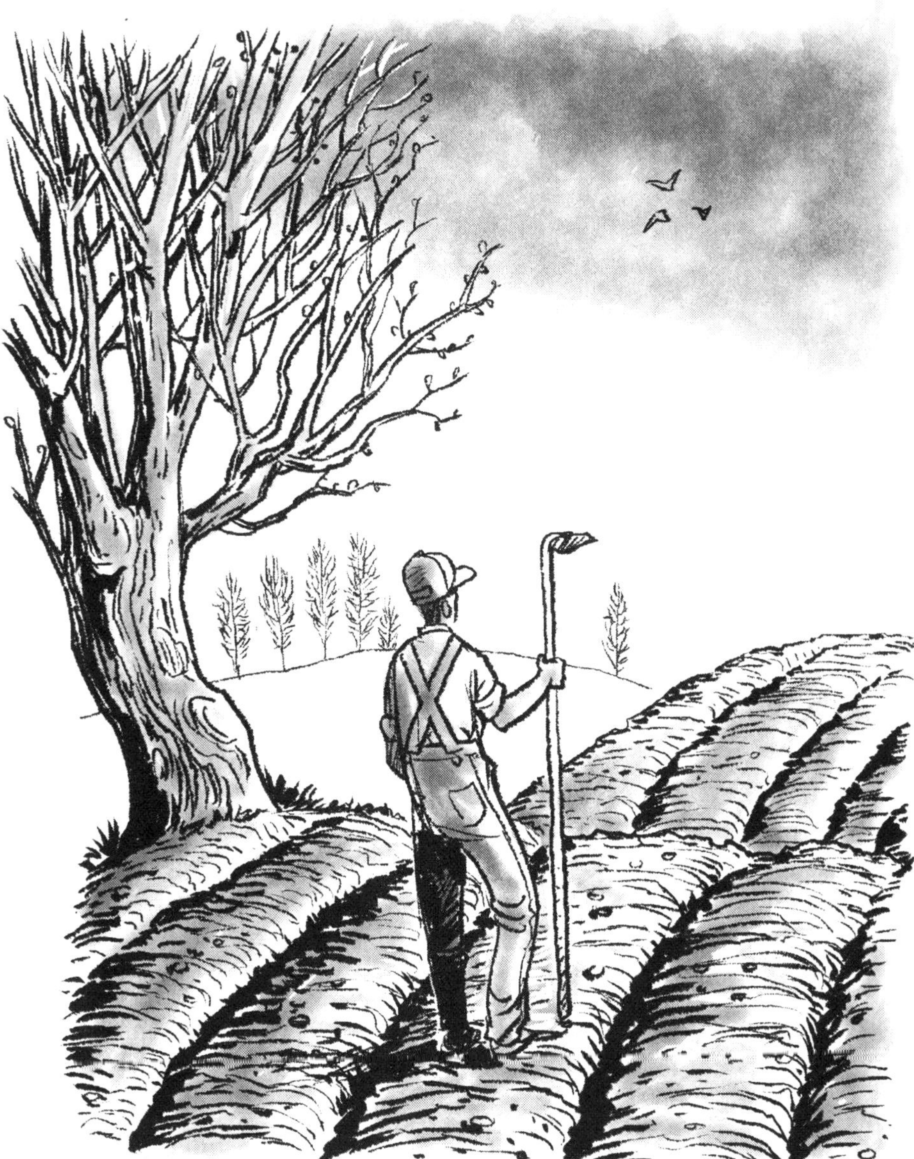

TEN

I'm a farmer who's been given a packet of seeds with no label, thought the Wanderer. What am I planting here? What will it look like? Will it be a small shoot or will it grow big? How do I take care of it? What do I look for? How do I tell the difference between weeds and the real thing? How much water will it take?

I can't do this. This will never work. I don't know what I'm doing.

The Wanderer looked at the small group of people gathered in his brother's house. The silence that hung over them was beyond awkward – it was suffocating. The Wanderer tried his best to fill up the space with conversation, but every attempt was met with minimal response. It was clear that everyone was wondering as much as the Wanderer what this was going to be.

His brother cradled a guitar on his knee, waiting to lead a few songs. His brother's wife, a young mother who had learned the artful technique of being present in two worlds at once, was physically with the adults but her ears were attentive to the noises of the children down the hall. The Wanderer's wife wore a similar look but because she was a guest in someone else's house, her attention was even more divided.

The single girl had come to the meeting because her friend from work had mentioned it. Her friend did not come.

The engaged girl, a friend of one of the Wanderer's friends, had heard about a Bible study and was hungry to learn about the Bible.

The young single man, invited by the single girl, wasn't sure why he was there.

This will never work, the Wanderer thought. What are we doing?

The Wanderer screwed up his courage and said, "Well, I guess it would be cool to just spend some time worshiping God together. Let's sing a few songs and just get our minds on Him. I know this is a little uncomfortable, but let's just see how the evening goes."

His brother led three songs. The Wanderer had hoped that maybe heaven would open during this time and some great sense of wonder and awe would envelope him and whisk him away into spiritual bliss, whisk him to an enlightened understanding of church simplicity. But all he noticed was a slight tingling sensation in his buttocks from sitting on a hard wooden chair.

The Wanderer got up and gathered a stack of papers he had set beside his chair. He walked around the room handing a sheet to each person. "I've put together a small Bible study. It's nothing much, just a few observations and questions about the Sermon on the Mount that I thought we could discuss."

This will never work.

The study never ended, the discussion led to one question after another. It was late and everyone needed to get home, so reluctantly, they called it quits. The women busied themselves with gathering up empty dessert plates and coffee cups. Hugs all around and final handshakes.

The single girl came to the Wanderer and said, "I really appreciate this. I feel like I learned a lot tonight. And I love the way we're doing this; it's just so relaxed and comfortable. I feel like I can be myself and still come to God. This is exactly what I've been looking for!"

The Wanderer watched as the last car drove away and stood in the glow of something that was brand new to him. This was real. This was simple.

This may work, the Wanderer thought.

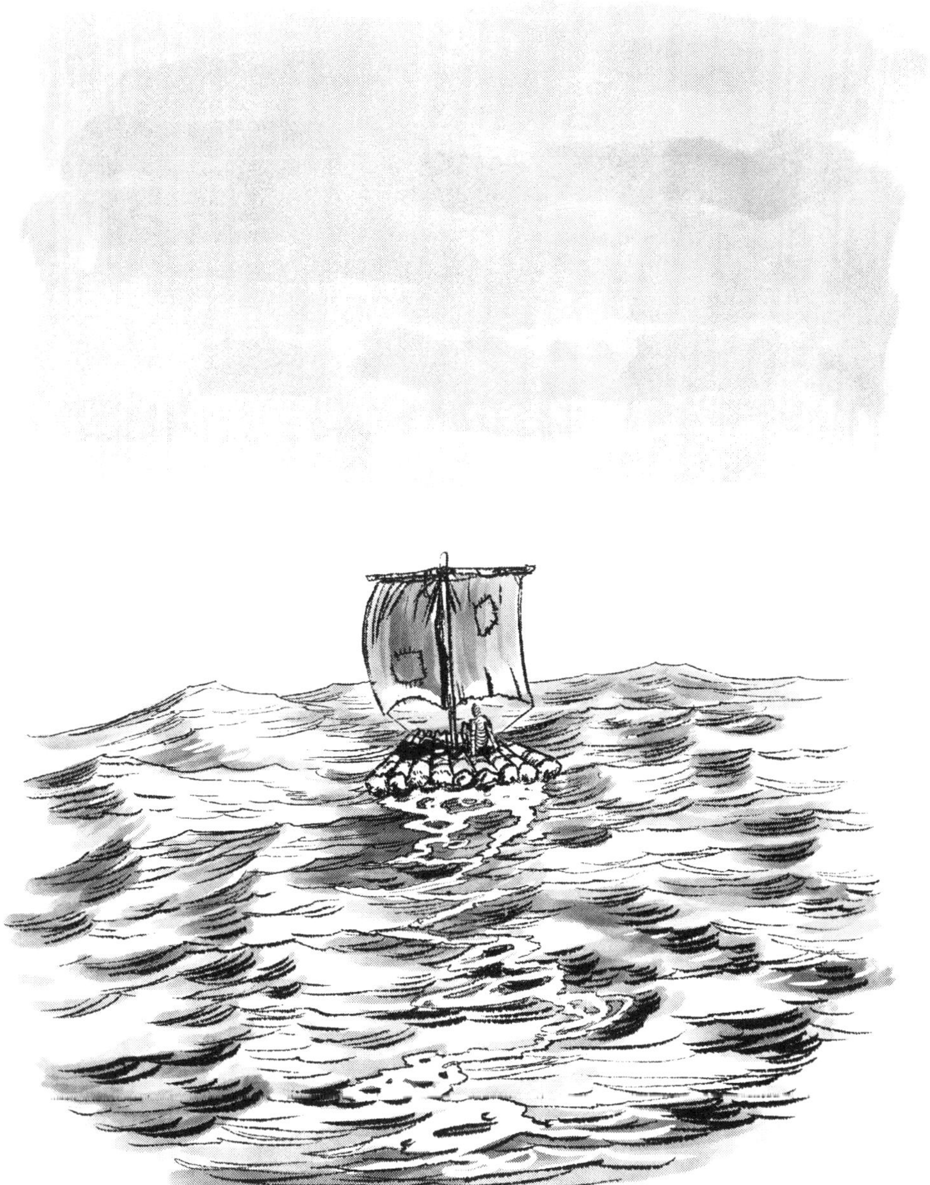

ELEVEN

The group looked at the Wanderer intently. He studied their faces, hoping he could read something that would indicate the right choice to make.

Eighteen adults were crammed into his tiny living room, a small band of dreamers who had set out with him on a journey away from church as they'd known it. They sat encircling the Wanderer, weighing out the news he'd just given them.

He continued talking, "Well, that's the bottom line. The pastor has decided to leave, and they are offering the building, chairs, and sound equipment for us if we want to move out of the living room and spread out in a larger meeting space."

"It is crowded here," said one person.

The Wanderer looked around at the people crammed into every free inch of space. "Yes it is."

The small group that had begun in his brother's home had moved to the Wanderer's house. He thought about how he and his wife had a running bet on which piece of furniture would get broken during the meeting. The sounds of kids wrestling tumbled down the hall from the children's bedrooms.

"It's a scary thought, but it's kind of exciting too," someone else offered.

"Who'll be paying the rent?" the Pragmatist asked.

"Good question," said the Wanderer. "I guess we'll have to start a community fund that will cover expenses like those."

"And what if nobody gives to this fund?" pressed the Pragmatist.

"Well, if nobody gives and we can't pay rent, then I guess we have our answer about whether we should have done this or not," the Wanderer said, trying to inject optimism into the conversation.

"So, this means we're going to start taking up offerings?" the Pragmatist added quickly.

"Why?"

No response.

"No, really, why would we need to do that? We all know there are needs. We all want to keep meeting together. Why would we need to act like we're not family and pass a bucket around like panhandlers? No, we will not be taking up offerings. We'll put a box or a basket or something out and people can contribute as they're led," the Wanderer said hopefully.

"So then, are we going to meet on Sundays now?"

"Maybe, maybe not. What do you guys think about Saturday nights? Leave Sunday open as a full day off to hang at the beach or whatever? It definitely would defy expectations!".

"I don't know. What if people think we're Sabbath observers? Or Jehovah's Witnesses?"

"People will think anything they want; we can't worry about that," someone else said. "I like the idea of a Sunday free-day!"

The group was getting more and more excited as they talked. They all prayed together, asking God for guidance, and spent some time in silence, contemplating the choice before them. In a unified decision, they agreed to assume the lease and take the equipment.

"Ok, one more thing," said the Pragmatist. "Does this mean we need to call you Pastor now? I mean, now that we're becoming a legitimate church?"

The Wanderer waited for the Pragmatist to chuckle or laugh, but the whole room had descended into a graveyard silence.

"Ok, let's start from the beginning again. A 'legitimate church'?" the Wanderer said, making quotation marks in the air with his fingers. "Let's go back to my manifesto. Why I hate church; part one–" The group cut him off with groans and laughter.

"You call me by my name and nothing else. We're in this together. You're not gonna' pin this whole rap on me!" the Wanderer said amid the laughter.

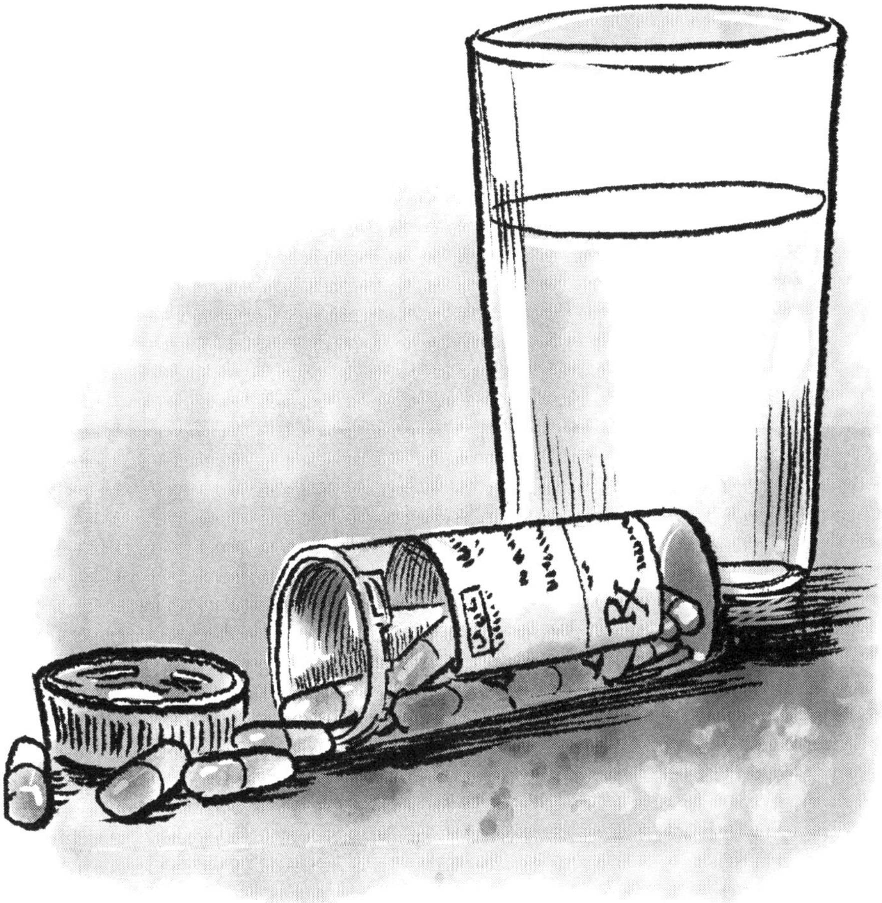

TWELVE

The few people in attendance had pulled the chairs into a semi-circle and sat facing one another. The Wanderer looked at everyone there, a group dwindled in number back to the size they were when meeting in his home. One of them was slurring his words and had the distinct odor of alcohol around him. Most of them had an air of disinterested obligation. Yet he knew from talking to most of them that they were hungry for God. It wasn't necessarily a failure on anyone's part.

It was seven o'clock on a Saturday night, and for the first time the Wanderer noticed how gloomy the rented room seemed.

It had been happening over a period of a few months. A malaise had slowly crept over the group. This was not something the Wanderer had anticipated. He felt as though this bold experiment was dying. He imagined this church as a child descending into sickness, growing weak and pale as he held her in his arms.

He was surprised to find how deeply connected and committed to this community he was. It had started with an attitude of waiting to see if it worked. Now that it wasn't working, the Wanderer was feeling a steady ache mounting in his chest.

Each week he'd look at one more empty seat which equaled one less personality in the mix. Excitement over something new had waned and flattened into a slow pulse.

He knew it had to do with meeting on Saturday nights. It was just too far out of normal expectations.

Like a steadily mounting drumbeat, he kept hearing people offer explanations: "We like this fellowship, it's just that we feel we need to be in a real church." He knew that "real" equated to a Sunday morning service according to cultural status quo.

The Wanderer stood at a crossroad. Setting out in the direction he had started in, this bold and exciting departure from all religious expectations clearly showed no signs of longevity. The alternative route presented his first encounter with compromise. Not a compromise of his core values, but a small concession to an infuriating subculture. Religious history had set the terms and his leverage was too infinitesimal to change the course.

The choice was like bile in his throat. It was more than a concession to him; it was an insulting loss. As simple as a change in schedule sounded on the surface, its effect on the Wanderer was that of a surprise uppercut that knocked him to the canvas. As though he could feel his opponent standing over him, smirking in contempt. "You'll meet when I say you'll meet. Your idealism will not withstand me."

It's time to quit, he thought. You gave it a good run; the old college try. Yet that appraisal scraped at his soul like a wire brush. How can I leave you? The image of a child, pale and deteriorating in his arms again filled his mind.

I want you to live, thought the Wanderer. What will it take?

When the realization dawned on him, he almost laughed out loud. What will it take? Fifteen hours. A change from seven o'clock at night to ten in the morning. Whose being legalistic now? Who cares when we meet? Is that really the issue I'd let this experiment conclude on?

It was an awakening moment. Who determined if there was a win or a loss? If grace was the bottom line, a change of schedule was an irrelevant issue. As though he were breaking out of a dense forest and finding an unexpected clearing, he considered: If that is irrelevant, what else is?

Following that line of intrigue, the Wanderer came to a jolting realization.

This is the outside edges of the machine he had been warned about. He had been maintaining that issues such as meeting times, dress codes or aesthetics were inconsequential. If that were true, then acquiescing to a cultural expectation was certainly not a crisis. If meeting times and schedules became the focus, negatively or positively, they could veer the community's course away from the heart of church. He could already see how a stubborn commitment to a schedule had drained the church and himself.

With a fresh new perspective and a reigniting of his original passion, he made a determination he decided to present at their next meeting.

"Tonight I have an announcement. I'm going to make an executive decision. That's not to say it's not open for discussion, but I really think we're at a place where some tough choices have to be made. I believe it's time to move our meeting to Sunday mornings again. We can keep doing this like we're doing and let this expire in the next month or so, or we can see what will happen if we become flexible and accommodate the cultural expectation of Sunday morning church meetings."

"Flexible, that reminds me, there's a yoga class I could attend if we didn't meet on Saturdays." said one of the young women in attendance.

"I think it's a great idea," ventured the alcohol man.

"It's time for a change," said the Pragmatist. "We need a change. Our hearts haven't been here. I was worried that maybe we were in over our heads, that maybe this was a mistake. But I agree, we should move the meeting to Sundays. I'm for anything that will shake this up."

The Wanderer smiled in response. "Me too. Well, let's go get something to eat. This is a good enough meeting for tonight. Next week be here Sunday morning at 10 o'clock for the relaunch. I'll bring the doughnuts. It'll be fun."

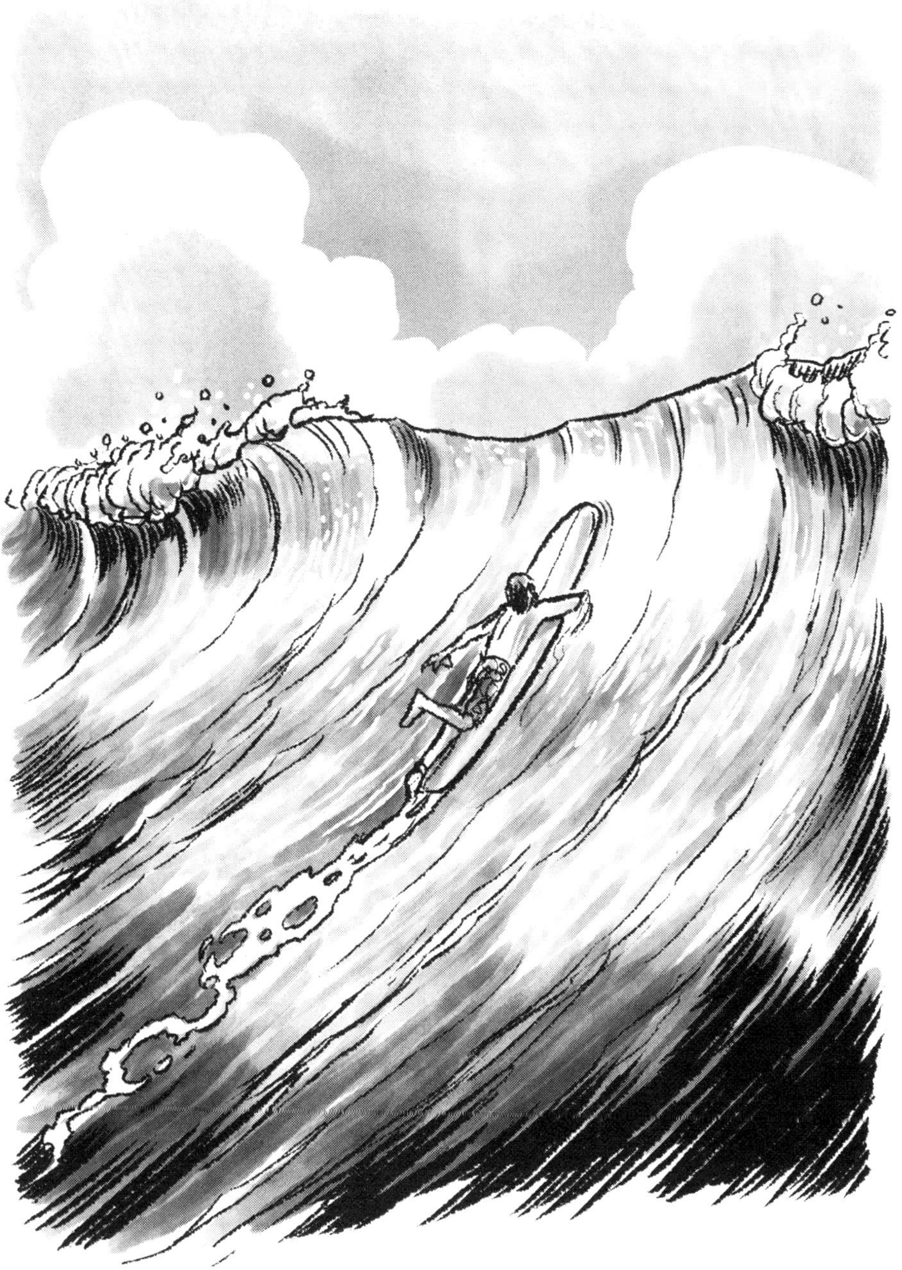

THIRTEEN

"If you become a 501-C3 tax exempt organization you're going to have to face some harsh realities my friend."

The Church Thug and his wife sat across from the Wanderer and his wife at the diner they had met in. The Church Thug smiled and shook his head like a man who was trying to inform a child about the facts of life. He dug his fork into his chicken fried steak and waited until his mouth was full to resume talking.

"We've learned a lot of hard lessons along the way. We used to be idealists just like yourself," the Church Thug said, holding his fork in one hand and pushing his glasses up onto the bridge of his nose with the other.

The Wanderer said nothing; he just looked at the soft, middle aged man with curly hair sitting across from him. Their conversation had been interrupted several times as the Church Thug took calls on his cell phone. The Church Thug's wife was mostly silent, never really looking up from her plate of salad. She would nod in agreement and only chime in to repeat something the Church Thug had said first.

"I'm just saying, people will let you down."

"They will let you down; it's true," she said.

A pastor whom the Wanderer felt he could trust had arranged this meeting. The Wanderer had expressed his dismay at navigating the process of filing for tax-exempt status and had asked for advice. The Wanderer was wondering if he'd been set up.

It had started out all right. In getting to know each other, they had exchanged small talk, divulging shared interests and points of view. But as the Wanderer began to unfold his particular vision for how a church could be, the conversation took a decidedly different direction in tone.

It was quite evident that the Church Thug did not agree with the Wanderer on the finer points of simplifying church structure. And it was also clear that he now felt it was his obligation to set the Wanderer straight.

The Church Thug took another bite of his dinner and leaned in across the table, scrutinizing the Wanderer. "This little endeavor of yours sounds really nice," he said with a patronizing smile. "But I'm here to tell you that it's not realistic in the least."

"How so?" asked The Wanderer as he finished up his plate of food, put down his fork and pushed his plate to the side.

"Dividing up leadership, keeping no membership and not taking up offerings, just for a start. Things just don't work that way," he said with a derisive chuckle. "I'm tellin' you, people will let you down. You're assuming too much about what church people are willing to do and give. If you don't call the shots and warn them to toe the line, they won't. They just flat won't!"

"They just flat won't!" his wife echoed.

The Wanderer never took his eyes off the Church Thug. All he had wanted was a little bit of practical advice, but like everything else he had discovered along the way, this too came at a price. The Wanderer could feel his face flushing and his eyes watering. He wished he could hide his frustration and embarrassment. He hated feeling so transparent.

The Church Thug continued, "I realize that this is hard news to take, but son, you've got to face it. All the stuff that's spiritual and uplifting about church is like, well, it's like advertising. It's the stuff we want everyone to see and appreciate about church, but there's more to it than that. You've got to face it son, there is a dark underbelly to the church that idealists like yourself don't like to acknowledge. But it's there, yes sir', it's there."

He leaned in even closer and stopped chewing. "You have got to realize that the church is first and foremost a business, and you have to treat it like that. You have to think about revenue and expansion or your little endeavor will just flat out fail. You better take what I'm saying seriously and save yourself and your family a lot of trouble."

The Wanderer never looked away and consciously tried to steady his breathing. He was mad, most of all with himself, that he couldn't hide his emotions better. He could feel a full-fledged tear rolling down his cheek, but he didn't announce it by wiping at it. Let it roll, he thought, maybe it will go unseen.

He had formulated his response while the Church Thug had looked away to scoop the last of his mashed potatoes into his mouth. When the Thug looked up from his plate, the Wanderer said, "Maybe you're right, but I'm counting on you being wrong. One thing I know for sure: If you are right, then I won't have anything to do with church ever again. If the church has to think like you and look the way you describe it, then I will walk away and never look back again."

The Wanderer got up, his wife following, and grabbed the bill from the middle of the table.

"Thanks for your time. I do realize you were trying to help." he said and walked to the register to pay the bill, then headed out into the cool evening air.

"Can you believe that guy?" the Wanderer's wife exploded. "Who does he think he is, the Pope?" They got into the car and the Wanderer saw his reflection in the rear-view mirror. His cheek was stained with the streak of the tear he had so stubbornly refused to acknowledge. Just past his own face in the mirror, the Church Thug and his wife were laughing about something as they entered their own vehicle.

"It's either real or it's not." He started the engine and slammed the car into gear moving quickly to the parking lot exit.

"I mean, church is either really supposed to be here by God's design, or it's not. I'm not sure it is real for that guy, so he's had to manufacture something that will stand in place of church. I think there are a lot of people who do that. But I can't. I won't. It's either real and going to be real, or it's not, and I'm done."

The Church Thug and his wife eased out of their parking space, pulling up behind them at the exit.

"It is real; you'll see," said the Wanderer quietly.

The dinner meeting echoed into the Wanderer's week. Like a callous on his foot, it tried to hobble his steps but eventually faded and flattened. It would be years before he thought of that conversation again. Driving home from a family trip, taking a different route than usual, the Wanderer would find the Church Thug's building, built from the ground with sound business tactics, empty and abandoned.

Weeds grew up along the edges of the structure and decorated the cracks in the parking lot. Full sheets of plywood covered the glass doors at the entrance. The amount of weathering they showed indicated that the building had been unoccupied for quite some time.

A large sign announced in big red letters: For Sale.

"It's either real or it's not," whispered the Wanderer as he watched the building disappear in his rear view mirror.

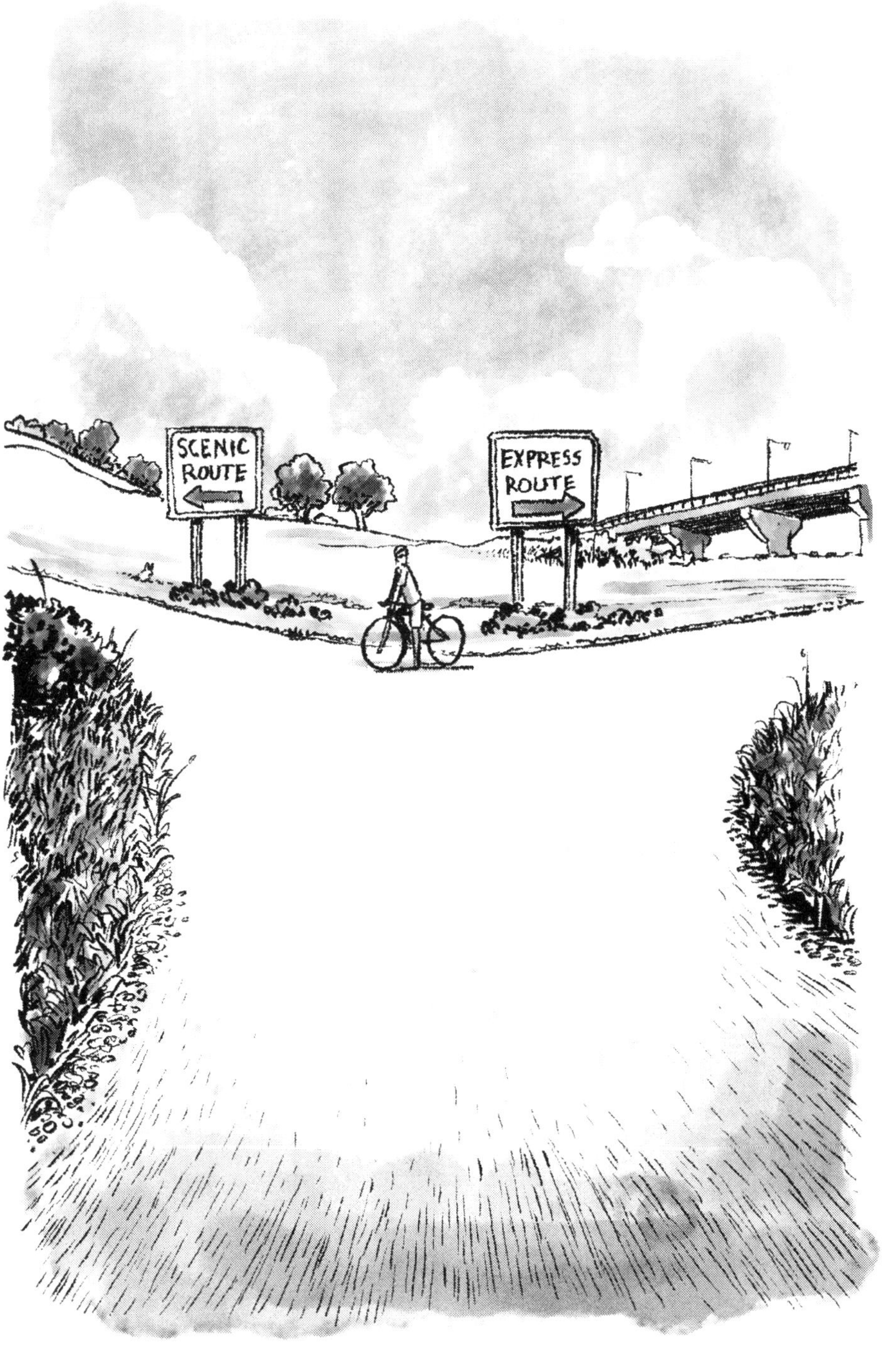
SCENIC ROUTE
EXPRESS ROUTE

FOURTEEN

The room was located in a long-forgotten, upscale mall. At one time, the unit had functioned as a dress shop. Mirrors covered the walls and the floor was a mixture of black and white tiles and rattan thatch. It was small and the ceilings were low.

The Wanderer surveyed the place, scrutinizing its details. There weren't, in fact, many details to examine, and that was the first problem he considered.

When people were coming to my house, they were getting to know me, he thought. Decorations, family photos collectible toys and books cover my house. It's part of the process of how people get to know me. When we met in a home, it was personal; it was interesting; and it exuded the warmth of life.

This room was cold to him, clean and orderly and boring. Seventy five black, stackable chairs donated by the Holiday Inn lined from the front to the back of the room. Everything in the space was black and white. The only exception was the rattan floor and thatch which the previous tenants had used to cover the mirrors on the walls to help with the off-putting, funhouse effect of walking into a room full of reflections.

The thatch stretched from floor to ceiling, so that the space emanated the sense of a tentative tiki bar.

"Makes me think of Gilligan's Island," he said out loud. "Which fits since we're a bunch of castaways from church." He smiled at his own remark, but slowly, what he had just said began to dawn on him. He imagined a whole spectrum of ways in which the room could be decorated to indicate the personality of the group who met there. Images from his childhood: The Mickey Mouse Club, the Monkee's Pad and the Little Rascal's meeting room.

"The church is a club! It's a hang-out for people who love Jesus!" he said, almost shouting. "Why shouldn't the place where it meets look like a clubhouse? Why shouldn't it be a place where you can be yourself and feel relaxed?" In his mind he began making contrasts. He compared his emotional reaction to a typical church setting, which their current space tried to imitate on a small scale, with a restaurant like Applebee's. Applebee's décor and style created an atmosphere that drew a person into a sense of casual comfort. A typical church setting, including their present room, did the opposite.

He scrounged around the room to find a piece of paper and a pen and began scratching down his thoughts.

When we come to Jesus, we're coming home. Where we meet should reflect the comfort of home.

Church is a family. We meet like a family… in a FAMILY room.

He walked around to the front of the room to face the rows of chairs, set up like pews. "When I call my family together to talk with them, I don't line them up in rows." He said to one of the empty chairs.

"They flop around on any seat around me or stretch out on the-" the Wanderer cocked his head with a smile. He moved through the room like a madman, pushing chairs around and rearranging the room.

He stood in one empty spot on the side of the space and looked around. "This would be a perfect place for a couch," A splash of dried coffee stained the rattan floor near his foot. "People need a place to rest their coffee cups. We need tables."

He ran out to his car and retrieved the surfboard he had been using earlier that morning. He brought it into the room and leaned it against the front wall, running his hand across the bumps of wax on the surfboard's deck, breathing in its bubblegum scent. He stepped back to observe the contrast of the blue and yellow painted design on the board with the thatch behind it. The board broke up the monotony of the wall and conveyed a style that rightly represented the beach culture where the church's space was located.

"I think we've got something here," he said.

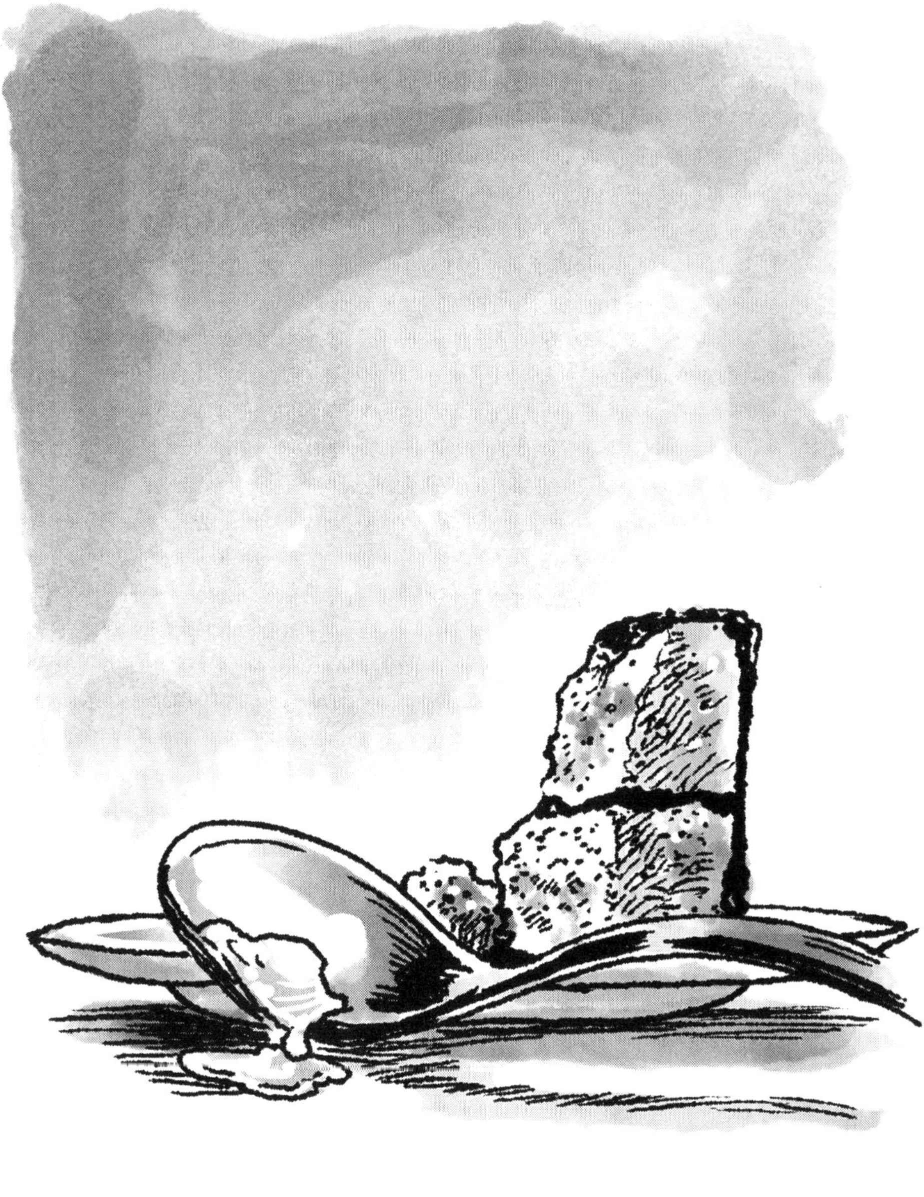

FIFTEEN

The Wanderer looked at the men and women who had gathered with him, who shared the leadership of the church with him. They were good people, and he trusted them without boundaries. Now they sat around him, looking at him earnestly and waiting for his response. But all the Wanderer could do was look at these friends of his and admire them.

There was the Cop, stocky in build and personality. His honesty and practicality were immeasurably important to the Wanderer. There was the Cop's wife, who presented a perfect balance of nurture and organizational skills. There was the Electrician, whose large frame contained one of the most confident people the Wanderer had ever met. For the Wanderer, that confidence was something he would lean into when searching for his own strength. There was the Electrician's wife whose calm sincerity felt like unseen ropes that held them all together. He looked at all the people gathered around him: the Salesman, the Wanderer's brother, the Intellectual. They shared his vision, they had given their hearts and minds and strength to the cause of finding a different way to do church. He loved them all.

What wonderful people to have as friends, he thought.

"Seriously, we need to decide what to do here," the Cop said. The Wanderer drifted back to his present reality.

"We are out of room, and this doesn't seem to be a problem that will go away."

"Do you realize that the kids are having to sit on the floor pretty regularly now?"

"It's really time to get serious about finding a new place to meet."

Chinese lanterns hung from the ceiling, and surfboards hung on the walls. There were posters and photographs and poems affixed randomly on the walls. The faint smell of coffee permeated everything. This was their hangout. This was the community's home.

"How would we ever duplicate this?" the Wanderer said, more to himself than those with him.

"Well, we wouldn't duplicate it. We'd just make it ours as we go," his wife said.

At her words the Wanderer sat up straight in his chair. This was serious. This wasn't one of the friendly, joking banters about how to become a mega church and buy him a jet. This was a full-fledged intervention, and he was the target of their concern. They were serious in trying to convince him that it was time to leave – time to leave the place where they had seen this community experiment work. This wasn't like going from the living room to the dress shop. The dress shop was just an oversized living room anyway. They were talking about doubling their space, moving far beyond the size of a homey room.

"Do you really think more than a hundred people would actually get involved in this thing?" he laughed, hoping they would see the ludicrousness of that notion.

To his horror, none of them had even the hint of a smile.

The Electrician's wife, soft-spoken and meek, finally spoke up. "You've been saying that all along. You always think we won't get any larger as a fellowship and this thing just never stops growing. If this is really about people and God is really in charge of it, then you've got to quit trying to manage it and control it and stunt its growth. This is natural; it's really a good thing if you'd just look at it properly. We haven't been marketing or manipulating people to get involved in this. This is just happening. God must be doing it and it must be meeting people's needs. You've got to let go of this and let God do what He wants!"

The Wanderer blinked. He knew how good her heart was. Worst of all, he knew she was right.

"I don't know guys. Can we even afford moving to a bigger place?" the Wanderer pleaded.

The eye rolls, disbelieving laughter and sighs from his friends told him his answer. It was a familiar symphony by now.

"Couldn't we just figure out a way to keep from becoming such a big community?" he was scrambling.

Silence.

"I mean, maybe we should start taking up offerings? Or I could teach on tithing for six months straight? That should scare people off!" Everyone laughed but no one agreed.

"Well, do we have any prospects to investigate? And who's going to be in charge of negotiating a lease when we find a place?"

The energy of the conversation grew and his friends spoke with great, animated gestures as they described how a new meeting place could be designed to fit their current needs. He knew they were right, and he loved this small group with all of his heart. This was cake and ice-cream. They were an intimate band of adventurers, exploring a whole new landscape. A bigger building meant more personalities and a whole new dynamic. Cake and ice cream was done. It was time to eat his peas and do the hard work of forging a larger community.

The Wanderer watched with melancholy affection as the beginning of the end dawned for the Wanderers first great clubhouse.

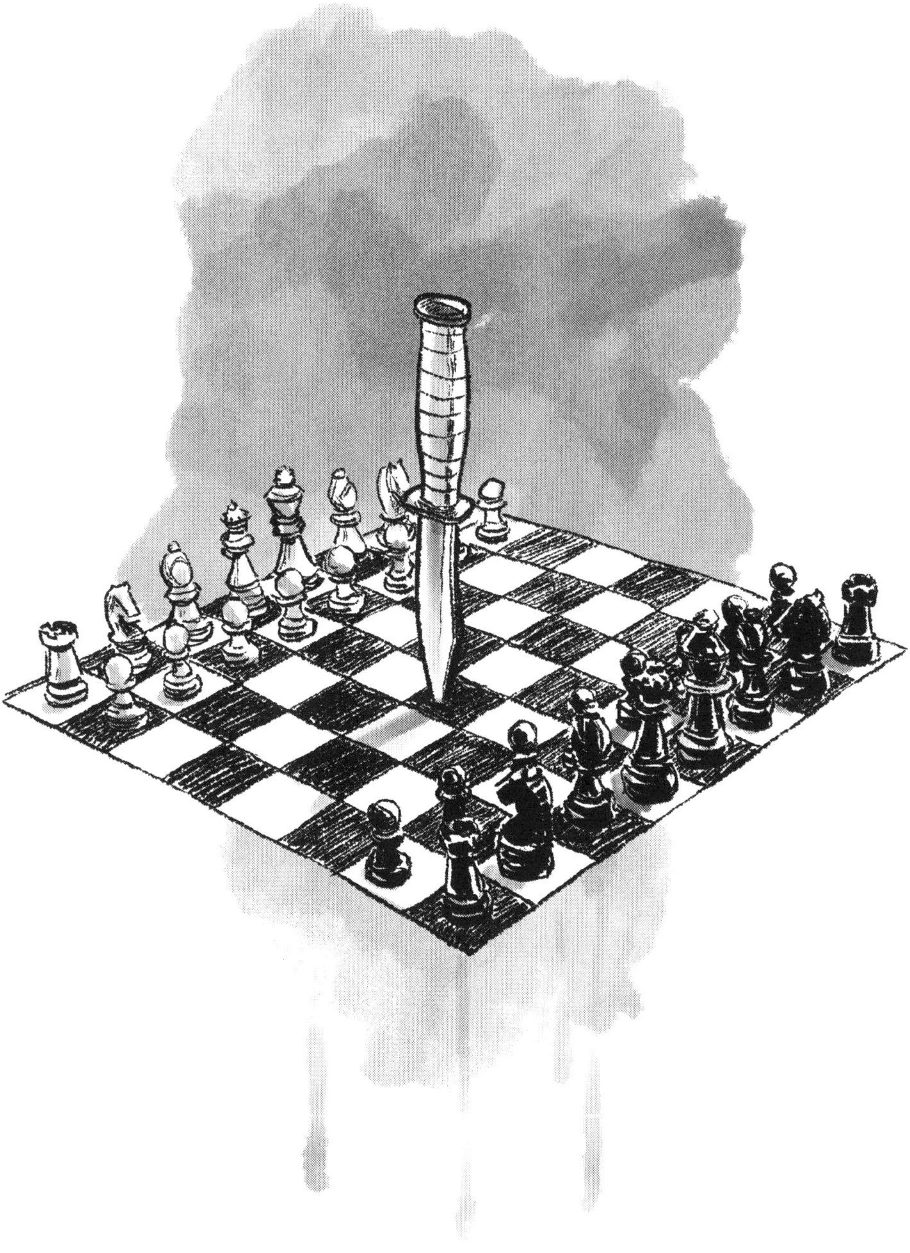

SIXTEEN

"So, I hear you have a little church meeting in this place."

"Uh, yeah, we sure do. Is there something I can help you with?" The Wanderer was standing outside of the building they had rented after leaving the dress shop, working on cleaning some patio furniture to put out front. The man standing before him was tall, in his late fifties with hawkish features and narrow eyes. He wore a light blue polo shirt and khaki pants, the uniform of those who must be forced into donning casual attire.

"What kind of church is this?"

It wasn't so much what he asked as it was the way he asked it. The Wanderer was tipped off as to who this man was. He knew this kind of question well, and it wasn't a pleasant inquiry but more like being slapped with a glove and invited to a duel. The Wanderer restrained himself from letting out a sigh.

He wanted to turn away, get back to what he was doing, pretend the man wasn't there. But none of those actions would pass muster with his conscience. He was trapped in the web of his own courtesy. The Church Spy had him and there was no escape.

"What kind of church is this?" the Wanderer repeated the question, buying himself some time. He knew what this question really meant: "What makes you think you're special enough to do this? What is your angle?"

The Wanderer knew by now that it was best to play things safe in these exchanges. "We don't belong to any denomination, if that's what you mean."

"So, you're independent," the Church Spy said matter-of-factly. "You're the pastor?"

"Uh, well, yeah I serve here and do most of the teaching, so yeah, I'm a pastor here," said the Wanderer, as though trying to convince himself.

"How many members do you have?" asked the Church Spy, looking past the Wanderer's shoulder, through the window into the Big Room, where the tables, chairs, couches and surfboards formed a cornucopia of uncommon comfort.

The Wanderer smiled at this question. Members were currency in church-speak. The membership numbers gave church leaders immediate readings about the value and status of a church and especially its leader. It was almost like a gauge on a leader's forehead which his peers would look at and measure his worth in the kingdom of God. Every leader he had ever known abided by this unspoken rule. If a leader had a lot of members, he was important and his work was "blessed." If he had very few, it must be a test, or there is something he must be failing to do, something about him that diminishes his worth. Every leader he had ever known always asked the question, "How are things at your church?" and every leader he had ever known always knew that that question really meant, "How many members do you have now?"

The Wanderer smiled, because he loved disrupting this game. It was childish and self-gratifying, but it was a temptation he could never resist.

"You mean, how many members on our official roll?" the Wanderer asked.

"Well, sure," replied the Church Spy.

"None," said the Wanderer, unable to suppress his smile.

The Church Spy cocked his head to one side like a man trying to understand someone speaking in an alien language.

"We don't have an official membership. We're just a bunch of friends hanging out and loving Jesus. People come and people go, and we assume it's all by God's leading." The Wanderer's teeth were showing his smile was so broad. In his mind, he said: Sorry pal, we just don't deal in the same currency.

"Oh, I see," said the Church Spy and the Wanderer read those three words like a speech. "Oh, I see, you are trying to avoid the game. You're a rebel; you're a flash in the pan. You try on different language, talking about friends instead of members, but I'm not impressed. I've been around; I've seen your type sprout up and die just as quickly. You are the fringe and on the fringe you'll always be."

"So, how many friends would you say hang out here?" asked the Church Spy, emphasizing the words "friends" and "hang out" with more than a trace of condescension.

"I couldn't say for sure; I've never counted personally." The Wanderer knew his attitude had taken a bad turn during this encounter and this discussion was fast becoming a religious pissing contest. "But, if you really are in need of a number, let's see, we have two hundred chairs in the Big Room plus couches, two services on Sunday morning that are just about full each time… So my guess would be close to four hundred friends."

He regretted it as soon as he said it.

"Really? I see," said the Church Spy, barely concealing his surprise. And in those two words the Wanderer read a different speech. "I see, you are, in reality, a threat. You are undermining the way things are done. You have no respect for order or history; you are a communist, a radical, a terrorist. You are suspect and will always be suspect."

In a sage-to-student tone, the Church Spy said, "That's a lot of people. It's a big responsibility."

The Wanderer was tired and sorry that he'd taken the conversation down this path. What did it matter, why not play by the rules? How did he really know what the man was intending in his questions? In a few hours, it would all have been forgotten and the bitterness of swallowing his pride would have worn off. His mind traced over so many of these same kinds of encounters, and all of them seemed to press on him, to wear him down.

"How do you expect to be blessed if you don't teach tithing?"

"How do you keep track of people's membership without providing a letter?"

"How do you make church decisions if you don't vote on them?" - "Well, we have a group of leaders who discuss issues, and after a lot of laughter and prayer, in that order, we either all agree or we don't do anything."

"How can you call yourself a teacher when you haven't been to seminary?" - "I don't know. Can I call a lifeline?"

"Is this a Spirit-filled church? Do ya'll have the Holy Ghost?" - "Is there such a thing as a church without the Holy Spirit? Wouldn't that almost be a contradiction in terms?"

The Wanderer's shoulders sagged as he put down the cloth he was using to clean the patio furniture. He dragged his head upward to see the Church Spy leaning into the glass to study the darkened room, muttering to himself, "A big responsibility."

"You know, it's really not that big of a deal. We're just broken people who have found a way to meet together that seems to fit our needs. We don't say it's the only way or anything like that. It's just our way and Jesus seems to heal us through it. I know it's not everybody's cup of tea and I wouldn't expect anyone else to do things the same way," the Wanderer said, hoping to find a gate in the fence between them.

"Yes, well, there are a lot of different views out there, that's true." The Church Spy held out his hand to shake the Wanderer's.

"Thanks for your time. Maybe we'll drop by sometime and visit with you," said the Church Spy as he loosely shook the Wanderers hand.

"That'd be great," said the Wanderer, knowing he would probably never see him again.

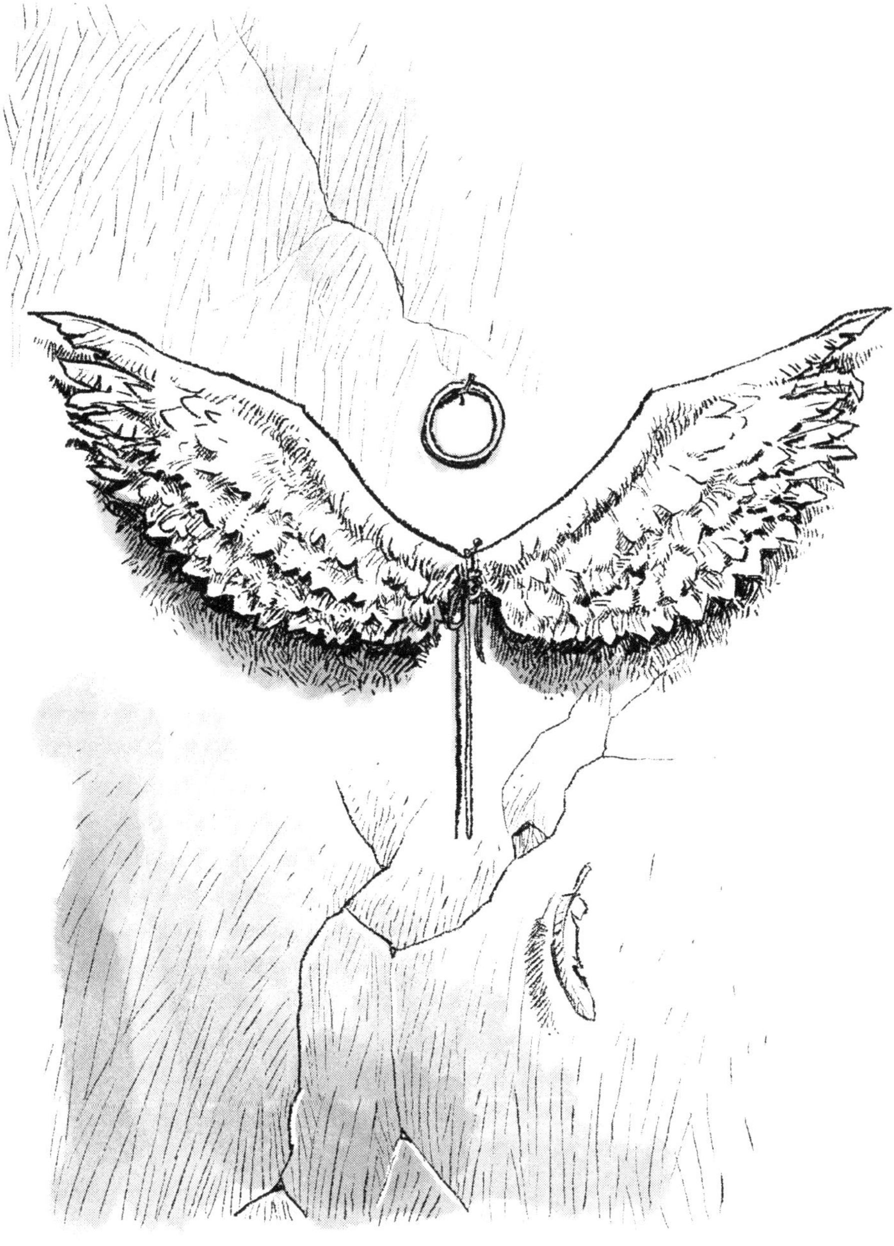

SEVENTEEN

From his office window, the Wanderer looked across the courtyard and watched two leather-clad bikers hold the door for an elderly couple as they entered the Big Room.

"I got an e-mail from a young guy who won't be hanging out with our church anymore," he said, almost absently to his brother who sat in the chair by his desk.

"Really? Why's that?" his brother asked.

Several middle school kids chased each other into the main entrance, followed by a single mom with two kids in tow. "He said that, well, I can't remember his exact words, but in essence he explained that he just couldn't handle a structured, organizational church anymore, so he's off looking for something different. A different way to do church."

"Organized, us? He's talking about this church?" stammered his brother in genuine surprise.

"Well, yeah. The e-mail was directed to me so I assumed it was about us."

"We played a dirge; we piped a tune for cryin' out loud, and there's just no pleasing some people," said his brother, who slumped down in his chair as though the weight of this news were pinning him there.

"It doesn't matter. I understand what he's saying. I mean, he is me fourteen years ago. He's looking for that ineffable something in church. A fleeting thought, a vision in the peripheral view. I wrote him back and told him he'll find it, and God will do cool things through him in the process."

The Wanderer smiled as he absently watched the people who continued to pass through the entrance to the Big Room. A young man he knew who struggled with anxiety was walking with a professional couple who had just moved to the state. He watched as they spoke to each other; he couldn't hear their words but the three smiles conveyed the tenor of their exchange.

"I found it, you know," he said, still watching the unusual comrades across the court.

"Found what?" asked his brother, staring at the floor.

"Wonderwhat. I found wonderwhat."

"Wonder…what? What are you talking about?"

"I've been wandering around the religious landscape for years, looking for something I couldn't clearly define, searching for some elusive expression of church. You know, the right way to do church – my wonderwhat." The Wanderer turned from the window and picked up a pen and tapped it on his desk. "But after all these years I realize I've found it."

His brother tilted his head and asked, "Well, what is it?"

The Wanderer was silent for a moment. His brother inclined his head in anticipation of the answer.

"I was so frustrated when I looked into the New Testament to find a description of the church only to realize it wasn't there. I just couldn't understand why God would have left that important bit of information out, you know, about how to do church. Something that important should have had a formula attached to it somehow. But it didn't.

"I think I understand now why it isn't described, because it's not about how to do church. It never has been. I think a church could meet, and it could use High-Church liturgies or just be random, casual get togethers. It just really wouldn't matter.

"What I was looking for, the reality I was craving, wasn't in a church style at all. What I was looking for was you, and your wife. And the cop and his family, and the electrician and his. And the vet and the carpenter and the student and the single mom and her kids and on and on and on. It was all of us, together on this journey, and the story that it tells.

"Church styles will come and go depending on the surrounding culture. What's really important is how we love each other and how our stories intertwine as we go along. That's where we find reality. When I ran away from church as I knew it, I thought it was the structure I was so offended by, but now I don't really think it was. I think it was the way we prioritized the structure over people.

The structure would have been fine as long as we understood its place – as something that serves people instead of the other way around.

"Emerging churches face the same danger that modern churches did if we focus on style or theologies or philosophies or deconstruction. Those things are okay as long as they stay in their place. Our church has a structure; the kid in the e-mail was right. But as long as we know what really matters are people, the structure is a secondary issue. As long as we are always willing to sacrifice any part of our structure in order to meet people's needs then I think we have church the way it was intended.

"Wonderwhat was not so much a how-to thing. It was about priorities. It was about relationships, family, and community. That's why the Bible didn't describe how to do that. You don't describe those things; you live them."

"Wonderwhat," The Wanderer's brother half mumbled as he shook his head. "So, what you're saying is, we could take those surfboards down, paint the walls white and play Bluegrass music during worship and that would still be okay?"

"Absolutely! It's just that I wouldn't be here with you," the Wanderer said, throwing the pen at his brother.

"You just have no taste!"

"You're dull and boring!" the Wanderer laughed.

They sat quietly in the office for a moment until the Wanderer finally said, "It's almost eleven. Let's go live a little with the family."

They both walked through the door and the Wanderer flipped off the light switch as they left. They walked across the courtyard toward the big room.

The Wanderer stopped and looked in the building where they had been meeting for several years, then turned his gaze toward the war vet and the recovering addict, the painter and the doctor, the young man with autism playing catch with the college student. A warmth spread across his chest and he knew he had made his way to the heart. He had found his home.

THE END

POSTSCRIPT

Ten years have elapsed since I first wrote the blog posts that would become this book. More than twenty years have slipped by since we first dared to carve out a space in the sacred province of churchdom. My children who were in grade school when we started now join me in attending the needs of ministry. Many gray hairs have replaced my youthful brown follicles – and many more cautious thoughts have supplanted what was a more innocent and youthful fervor.

Several parts of this work make me wince as I read them from a more experienced position in life. I may wish to word some things differently now; I may hold my tongue on some issues. Still, the deep discontentment I felt as a young man setting out on this journey still resonates in my present state.

So much has changed on the landscape of the American Evangelical Church from the time our adventure first began. The Emergent Church has come and gone and none of us were really sure what it was or where it went. Mega-churches with multiple satellite campuses have been on the steady march towards dominating our present conversations about ecclesiology. Casual is the new standard; rock shows are the new state of worship. A lot has changed.

My discontentment has not.

All too often it appears that what we've done is put a new haircut on the same old system. Subcultural expectations are still the norm. Controlling, abusive leaders still seem insulated and unchallenged in their positions of power, with only a few exceptions among the most visible of their kind. The "business" of the modern church still seems to take priority over the people who make up the family of God. I still encounter a steady stream of outcasts who were sacrificed on the altar of respectability.

I wish I could say that we discovered the hidden key that turns all of that around; the map that leads to community in a perfect state. We have not. The values we set out with are still largely intact. Many of the same people with whom we started this journey are still in community with us today.

We've added new friends and lost some old ones. We learned many painful lessons along the way and uncovered unthinkable joys that we hadn't anticipated as well.

What I hadn't counted on has turned out to be the one constant struggle on this trail: the ongoing contest to retain simplicity. There is a forceful, consumer current that flows through our present culture that comes with robust expectations about service and performance. When that gust slams against a group of people who want to serve others, it results in a disquieted tension. "Should we be doing this? Do we need more of that?" The great temptation is to start adding and doing in order to meet consumer needs. Simplicity wants to squirm away in that contest, and we wrestle to hold on to her like Jacob wrestled with God. We often limp away accordingly.

Our intent was to develop a church community around the goal of learning how to love God as well as learning how to love people. Neither one of those goals is easy to do, but this is our story so far.

I certainly wouldn't hold up our church as a standard, but I'm not ashamed of her either. God has met us, corrected us, encouraged us and hopefully laughed with us over the years.

Here's hoping we have many more to come.

The Didache

An ancient start-up guide for church

Paraphrase by Rob Woodrum

THE DIDACHE PARAPHRASE

Introduction 85

THE ISSUES OF LIFE

Chapter 1   Duae Viae – The Two Ways 87

Chapter 2   Forbidden Activities 88

Chapter 3   Forbidden Attitudes 88

Chapter 4   Relationships, Temporal and Spiritual 90

Chapter 5   The Way of Death 91

Chapter 6   False Teachers and Lifestyle Issues 92

CHURCH ORDER AND PRACTICE

Chapter 7   Baptism 92

Chapter 8   Fasting and Prayer 93

Chapter 9   The Lord's Supper 93

Chapter 10 Thanksgiving After Communion 94

Chapter 11 How to Test Teachers, Apostles and Prophets 96

Chapter 12 How to Treat Strangers 97

Chapter 13 How to Take Care of Church Leaders 98

Chapter 14 Importance of Community Life 98

Chapter 15 How to Choose a Leader 99

Chapter 16 What We're Waiting For 99

INTRODUCTION TO THE DIDACHE:

GROPING IN THE PAST TO FIND OUR FUTURE

The didache (did-ah'-kay) is one of the earliest known non-canonical (something not considered to be part of the Bible) pieces of Christian literature. The word "didache" is Greek for "teaching" and it has traditionally been called the "Teaching of the Twelve Apostles." Early church writers such as Athanasius, Didymus and Eusebius (who wrote an ancient history of the early church) made references to this work, but no actual copy of the work was found until 1873. Greek, Coptic and Ethiopian fragments of this same document were found in later years.

Since its discovery this document has received a great amount of scrutiny and has proven to be as mysterious as it is insightful. The work is brief and appears to be, according to Athanasius, a sort of startup guide for new churches. It contains two sections: first, on Christian conduct and attitude, and secondly a manual on church order and practice. There is a brief apocalyptic note at the end which contains many similarities to apocalyptic references from the synoptic Gospels as well as Paul's didactic epistles. It has an inherent Jewish form of moral practice, which indicates its primary target audience was the emerging Jewish church.

We don't know who wrote it but tradition states that it was the instruction of the twelve apostles given to those who had come into the Christian faith.

While it's unlikely (according to those who know about such stuff) that the original twelve authored this, it is possible that it is the direct result of the first apostolic council found in Acts 15. Since the writing style varies from section to section it is considered to be a composite work (several authors writing it). There isn't enough evidence to definitively date the document but scholars who know about such stuff place it anywhere from 50 A.D. to as late as 150 A.D. The latest research seems to lean toward an earlier date, between 50 and 70 A.D., which would mean it was circulating at the same time the original gospels were being developed and circulated.

Why did I feel a need to write a paraphrase (a rewording, taken from J.B. Lightfoot's literal translation) of the Didache?

I firmly believe that if you want to get to the truth of a matter, you go back to its beginning. If this document was as old as some suggest and is the result of the first apostolic council, think of what that means! To be able to catch a glimpse of how the beginning church functioned, what its priorities were, and what its primary message was is an invaluable help to me. If this were a primer for how churches should be planted in the past, would it still be useful for understanding our function as the church today? I think so.

It's with that in mind that I felt it so beneficial to write, in basic, contemporary language the profound insights that this document provides for us who seek to know the why's and how's of church structure. I have done my best to stick to the basic tenor of what Lightfoot wrote in his literal translation. There are spots where I may be accused of editorializing, but for the most part, I tried to keep with a basic restructuring of each sentence into a more accessible language and cadence.

I have read and re-read this document and find a fresh awakening of hope for the innocence of the church each time. I can only trust that this work will somehow be beneficial to more than just myself.

THE ISSUES OF LIFE

1. "DUAE VIAE - THE TWO WAYS"

There are only two ways on this journey, one way is life, the other is death, and there is a world of difference between the two.

This is what the way of life is like: first and foremost, you must love the God who created you. This will, secondly, enable you to love your fellow man as much as you love yourself. Whatever you wouldn't want people to do to you, you definitely shouldn't do to other people.

Here's how we would put this teaching into words: Say good things about those who speak bad things about you. Offer up prayers, even skip a meal in fasting for the ones who are determined to be an enemy and treats you cruelly. What's the big deal if you love those who love you back? People who never even think about God behave that way. On the other hand, if you will extend love toward those who break your heart, you've got something, something that will win people over so your list of enemies begins to shrink.

Control yourself; keep your body's desires in check. If someone hits you in the face, don't hit back; present the cheek he didn't hit. Do this, and you will be complete in reflecting God's image. If someone takes advantage of you and stretches you to your limits, let it become an opportunity to live as a servant. And if someone steals your coat, give him your shirt as a present as well. If someone steals something of yours, don't even bother asking for it back because all that does is stir up more trouble.

Be generous in giving to anyone who asks and don't set up any repayment plans, don't even ask for anything in return. Your Father loves it when you give generously out of the abundance of blessing He has given you. Whoever gives like this is content and knows fulfillment, secure in one's standing before the Father.

But here's a warning: If a person is really suffering a lack in material resources, it's good and right to provide for him. However, its highly problematic if a person is receiving material blessings while his hand is already full. He's going to have to give an account for why he took more than he needed and his greed will cost him dearly. Such things don't escape our God's notice.

Here's an old saying that's a good piece of advice: "Don't be hasty in determining how to give. Hang on to your gift until your hand sweats; take your time in discerning who should receive it."

2. "FORBIDDEN ACTIVITIES"

Here's the second important thing to obey from this teaching. These are the things that we cannot participate in: murder, adultery, child molestation, sexual promiscuity, stealing, white or black magic, abortion or infanticide. No lusting after your neighbor's possessions, no lies about your neighbor to make yourself look good; in fact, don't say anything that isn't good in nature. Don't hang on to a grudge against someone.

Don't waffle in your decisions or pander to what someone wants to hear in hopes that you'll get something in return. That kind of talk is deadly. You must be a person of your word; if you say it, do it. And don't be greedy or hoard up material stuff. Don't pretend to be something you're not and don't be a hothead or arrogant. Don't ever conspire to do something against your fellow human being.

You mustn't hate any person. Now, some you'll have to correct and others you'll just have to pray for, but all in all, the goal is to love others more than your own life.

3. "FORBIDDEN ATTITUDES"

My child, you must simply run away from what you know is evil or even looks evil. Don't live out of anger because anger is the catalyst for murder. Jealousy, bickering, being hot-tempered, these aren't the things you want to live from because they're also the seedbed of murder.

My child, don't let lust run loose in your heart because from there it will find action in sexual immorality. Be careful with your speech; don't get in the habit of talking dirty. And watch your eyes; don't let them roam around looking for someone to lust after. These things will end up growing into a weed-bed of sexual sin if you allow for them.

My child, don't get caught up in psychic phenomena because that stuff leads to false worship practices. And stay away from any practice of magic or astrology, even if you say it's just for kicks; these kinds of things lead people to put their faith in false gods or false methods of spirituality.

My child, don't speak the language of lies, lying is just like stealing trust. Don't accumulate possessions out of selfish or arrogant greed because this is the motive behind theft.

My child, don't spend your day complaining because it won't take too long before you're complaining against God. Don't go chasing after your own will and don't spend your hours thinking about things you're unhappy with because these are the things that lead to a contempt for God's will.

Here's how you should live: Be a person whose strength is kept under God's control because one day, that kind of person is going to be the owner of everything that money can't buy. Be a person who can tolerate difficulty for a long time. Be a person who cares about others and who does something about it, not for how it makes you look but out of good motives. Don't be quick to blurt out whatever comes into your head but think about what you say and how it will affect others. You want to be a person who is respectful to the teaching you've heard.

Be a person who is content with being the little guy and not the celebrity. Be the bouncer at the entrance of your soul and keep over-confidence out. Be a person who hangs out with the good-hearted nobodies and don't just seek to rub shoulders with the upper-crust crowd.

Pay attention now, as you walk through this world and stupid things happen to you, realize that God is in control of everything that comes your way and He's got a plan that has your best in mind.

4. "RELATIONSHIPS, TEMPORAL AND SPIRITUAL"

My child, whether it's daytime or nighttime, be sure to pray for those who are teaching the Word of God to you. Be respectful to them because when the Word of God is being taught it's as though the Lord Himself is there speaking. Every day you should look for and be friends with those who are moving deeper in their relationship with the Lord; you can really find good support in that kind of company and conversation.

Unity is precious; don't do anything that would divide people from each other but actively work to keep everyone together in peace. If you find yourself needing to help mediate in a quarrel, do it impartially and according to what's right. Then you can stand firm in your decision in the confidence that comes from right thinking.

Don't always be on the receiving end of gifts and then suddenly have withered arms when it comes your turn to give. If you have money and goods passing through your hands be generous with it all. That kind of generosity reveals a heart ransomed from sin. Muttering under your breath as you give or clutching the dollar you reluctantly part with isn't the right way to give either. You need to remember you can't out-give God, the real Head of payroll. He's in charge of bonuses for those who give generously. Don't you dare turn a blind eye to your brother or sister when they're in need. Instead, look at them as a co-owner of everything you have. In reality, nothing is totally yours anyway. We are all co-owners of everything God gives spiritually, eternal salvation, so it only makes sense that temporal things should be considered community property as well.

Never neglect your responsibilities to your children. Not just for physical needs but teach them proper respect for God as well.

If you have employees don't give orders to them out of anger, especially if they're also Christians, because that could cause them to begin equating your authority with God's which rules you both. This could cause them to lose their right perspective and respect for God. God doesn't reach out to people based on a social pecking order but comes to men and women solely on their readiness to receive His Spirit.

If you're an employee be a really good employee, doing all your work as though you were doing it for God Himself. Be humble and respectful as you do it.

It's all right to hate playacting in spirituality, hypocrisy is a stain on the church. Hate everything that isn't in harmony with God's good character. Don't ever give up on seeking to know and do what the Lord wants you to do. Actively determine to do all the stuff you've been taught to do (without adding a lot of other condemning requirements or leaving off the things that seem too hard).

Be honest and real when you're with the church. If you blew it be willing to admit it. Don't hide your wrong attitudes or actions under the guise of prayer; listen to your conscience. Remember, this is the way of LIFE we're on.

5. "THE WAY OF DEATH"

In contrast, the way of death looks like this: it has a long laundry list of things that destroy. Its evil and cursed nature is right up front. On this path there is murder, adultery, lusts of all kinds, sexual promiscuity, theft, false religious loyalties, dark magic and demonic powers, robbery, slanderous lies, fake religious masks, deceptions, evil conspiracies, pride, perverted behavior, self-will, pig-headedness, greed, foul talking, selfish jealousy, and over confident boasting!

If someone is good or lives for the good, those on the way of death will often hate and hurt her. The Truth is hated as well but lies hold a special place in their heart. They can't even conceive of living this life with the world to come in view. They don't hold to anything good or approve of right choices. They wouldn't roll out of bed for something good but they'd work night and day for evil purposes. A patient, gentle mindset is like a distant idea, far from view.

If it's worthless, they love it all the more. They're only interested in how they can profit from any given thing. They turn a blind eye to the poor and wouldn't lift a finger to help someone in need and burdened down. Because they don't believe they're made in God's image they don't care about future generations and actively seek to spoil anything that reflects the good of God. They impassively walk away from those who are hungry or hurting, and instead lift up to celebrity status those who are well off and who have climbed to power by walking on the backs of the poor. They are altogether outside of God's plan.

May you, my dear children, be rescued from that sort of pathway.

6. "FALSE TEACHERS AND LIFESTYLE ISSUES"

Pay close attention to what you're being taught. Make sure you're being pointed toward God's good path and not some cheap substitute. Not to say that you'll be able to live out the truth perfectly, but live this out to the best of your ability. Concerning dietary issues, if it's a possibility, do your best to stay away from unclean food, that is, food that people associate with false worship practices. People are led astray by that dead stuff.

CHURCH ORDER AND PRACTICE

7. "BAPTISM"

Let's talk a little about the practice of baptism. Here's how you should carry this out:

> First, go over all this teaching and make sure the person being baptized is in agreement with it. Find some running water and immerse the person in the name of the Father, Son and Holy Spirit. If you can't find any streams or rivers, then find some other place where there is enough water to perform the ritual. It can be cold or warm; it doesn't matter.
>
> If you can't find sufficient water to immerse a person in then pour water on their head three times, in the name of the Father, Son and Holy Spirit.

Fasting would put the person doing the baptizing and the person being baptized in the right spiritual frame of mind. It's not a bad idea for anyone who's able to fast to do so before the ceremony. Really, the one being baptized should fast, even for a day or two leading up to this event.

8. "FASTING AND PRAYER"

When you do fast don't do it anything like the religious play actors out there. They're known for fasting according to the liturgical calendar, so it would be better if you fast on different days as you prepare for Sunday.

Certainly don't pray like those windbags, either. Instead, pray like Jesus taught us in His Good News. Here's how He taught us to pray:

> "Our Father who is in heaven, help us to live in awe of Your name.
>
> Let Your authority be the supreme rule here, set up Your good plan here on earth, the same way things are good in heaven.
>
> Provide for every meal we eat to keep us going.
>
> You have forgiven all the ways we betrayed You, help us to treat others the same way.
>
> Keep us safe from our own will and from our Enemy's lies, keep us away from everything that isn't good like You.
>
> You call all the shots, You have total control, Your beauty never, ever ends.
>
> All this I agree to as Truth!"

It would be a good practice to pray on these lines three times a day, morning, noon and night.

9. "THE LORD'S SUPPER"

Now, with regard to the celebration of the Lord's Supper, here is how you should pray:

First, as you consider the cup of wine, pray:

> "Oh Father, we so thank you for the Grapevine, woven through history; Your ongoing plan which was revealed in David's story but fulfilled through Your Son, Jesus.
>
> Your beauty and power never, ever ends!"

Then, as you consider the bread, pray:

> "Oh Father, we so thank you for a brand new life and a whole new way of understanding, given to us by Your Son, Jesus.
>
> Your beauty and power never, ever ends.
>
> Just like this bread we break was once wheat scattered in many fields but has come together as one loaf; so let us, Your church, come from the North, the South, the East and the West and be gathered together in unity under Your rule.
>
> Through Jesus, the One, Your beauty and power and rule never, ever ends!"

Be careful that everyone knows how serious this is. No one should be eating and drinking the Body and Blood of Jesus who hasn't surrendered their lives to Him.

Remember, Jesus told us this is the children's bread, don't just treat it as scraps you give a dog.

10. "Thanksgiving After Communion"

When you've finished eating and drinking at this celebration, here's what you should pray:

> "We thank you oh Father! You built a house in our hearts and you put Your name on it, even though You are so completely pure and we are not. We thank you for a new way of seeing things and for the great adventure of living without fully understanding and for a life that will never, ever end, because of Your Son Jesus.

Your beauty and power never, ever ends!

You are the all-powerful Artist who designed everything known and unknown, all because you enjoyed creating it! And You gave us food and drink that tastes so good, all so we would remember You and thank You as we enjoy it!

Best of all, you gave us spiritual food and drink, a life that never ends through Your Son.

To thank you and acknowledge Your rule over us becomes our number one priority!

Your beauty and power never, ever ends.

Keep the people you've called out of the world before Your eyes, Lord. Deliver them from everything that isn't good like You and form us together into a complete representation of Your love.

From the four corners of the world, let us all be drawn together, out of this world's system and into Your kingdom. That has been your plan all along.

Your beauty and power and rule never, ever ends!

Let Your relentless love and care come to us and let this broken world fade away.

Rescue us, oh God of David!

If anyone has switched his loyalties to God, come on in!

If anyone hasn't, you can still change your mind and do so. Maranatha – the King will return.

All this I agree to as Truth."

Now, if a person is moved by the Spirit to pray by God's leading, then, of course, let him do that as well

11. "How to Test Teachers, Apostles and Prophets"

If a person comes to teach you and what he teaches lines up with the teaching found here, then welcome him in and listen to him or her.

But if he comes with some "new" or alternate "truth," realize that he's veering you off way of life and is trying to drag you down the path of death! Plug your ears from that noise.

But if her teaching challenges you to be more like God who is good and aids you in your understanding about God's plan, then welcome her in as though the Lord himself is there.

Now, concerning the spokesmen and mouthpieces of the Lord, prophets who are traveling around, handle them in a way that is in harmony with God's values.

If a prophet, an ambassador with God's message comes to you, receive him just as though the Lord is right there with you.

He should only enjoy your hospitality for one day, maybe two if the situation calls for it. But if he seems content to hang out for three days, realize that you're dealing with a false prophet.

When a true spokesman for the Lord leaves your company he won't take anything from you except what supplies he would need to get him to his next destination. If he starts asking around for money, this guy's a false prophet.

If a prophet is giving a message by the Spirit that is clearly by the will of God, don't start second-guessing her motives or picking apart his words. This is treading too closely to doing what unbelievers do in disdaining the work of the Spirit, and we know that is a serious offense to God.

Be warned, just because a guy may give a prophecy doesn't mean he's a bona fide prophet; his life and priorities will bear that out.

Here are the ways you can tell the difference between true and false spokesmen for God:

If a spokesman of the Lord says he has a word by the Spirit that you should prepare a meal and then gobbles it all up himself, that guy is a false prophet.

And if she teaches you to follow and live out the truth of God's plan but she doesn't live it herself, she's obviously false too.

If a prophet has been proven to be a true spokesman for the Lord and yet he uses strange or weird illustrations, acting strangely in the process; don't let it concern you, unless he suggests that you have to be weird too. You don't need to judge that stuff. God will deal with all that when everything comes to the end.

If you think about it, the Old Testament prophets were pretty odd ducks, so it may just be a hazard of the job.

And if anyone tells you, supposedly by the Spirit, to give her money or goods of any kind, don't listen to a word she has to say. On the other hand, if she says by the Spirit to give on behalf of others who are in need, that's a different story. That could very well be a prompting to generosity by the Spirit.

12. "How to Treat Strangers"

Here's the principle: welcome and be hospitable to anyone who drops by who shares your same loyalty to the Lord. As you're around them, you'll get to know them and know if they are for real or not in their association with the Truth.

If a person is traveling through the area, help him out as much as you are able to but keep an eye on what he's doing; he shouldn't stay with you more than two or three days at the most.

If he likes your community and the area and wants to make it his home, he needs to have some skill or trade so he can get a job and support himself.

If he doesn't have a skill, you'll have to decide how he might be able to work to help the community in exchange for support; he can't just sit around and be fed.

If he's not willing to do some work around the place, then he's a swindler who's learned how to use Christ's name to get a handout.

It's unfortunate, but you'll have to watch out for individuals like that.

13. "How to Take Care of Church Leaders"

If a spokesman for the Lord wants to settle down in your area and be a part of your community, take care of his needs and provide for him because your community needs him. That ends up being the work he does for you.

The same would be true for a teacher. If she's a good teacher who helps you understand God's good plan, she's someone you need; you should provide for her needs.

You can carry out the same principle from the Law where the first part of all the harvest and oil and wine, as well as the first born of the livestock were given to the high priest. You could follow that pattern for the prophet who is living with you.

And if you don't have a prophet/spokesman as part of your community, you could follow that pattern and give that stuff to the poor people in the neighborhood.

You could follow this principle through every part of your livelihood and give away everything that comes off the top, just like they did under Moses' law.

14. "Importance of Community Life"

On Sunday, get everyone together to share a meal and thank God. Be honest and real with each other about your failures and weaknesses.

You want this to be real spirituality, not just a religious show.

And if there's a feud going on between two people, don't let their lousy attitudes spoil the whole party. Make them wait outside until they can get things reconciled and behave like adults.

This is the kind of worship and sacrifice the Lord has always been looking for. Remember what He said:

> "In all places, at all times, give Me real worship and loyalty. The Lord reveals that He is the One and only King and His name is better than anything else on earth!"

15. "How to Choose a Leader"

Your community should choose as leaders people who are good with administration and people who have a heart to serve you. People whose lives reflect a harmony with God's character and who aren't in it for the money; people who have proven over time that they can be trusted.

These people will serve you in the same capacity as the prophets and the teachers do.

Show respect for these people, they are just as deserving of respect as prophets and teachers. What they provide for your community is just as good as what prophets and teachers provide.

Each of you should take on the responsibility to watch out for each other and correct each other if need be. Not because you're mad at someone but because you care and want peace for her or him, just like you were instructed to do in God's good plan.

Don't be an enabler or try to reason with someone who is abusing another person. Back off from them until they see the need to stop behaving that way; that's the only real help you can give them.

Let your prayer life, your gift giving and your whole life be harmonious with all you've learned from God's good plan.

16. "What We're Waiting For"

Be careful about how you're living. Let your light shine brightly and keep your armor in place, living in a way that you're ready for the unexpected return of the King.

Get together as often as you can, because your highest priority should be what's best for your inner person.

Remember, this whole journey you've been on and all that you've experienced won't mean a thing if you give up on the last stretch.

When this world is close to taking its last breath there will be tons of people who present a counterfeit truth, who spread their lie like a computer virus, corrupting every good thing. Those we thought were true sheep will, in the dying light, be revealed as wolves. People will forget what love is, much less how to live it, yet will be ingenious in finding new ways to hate.

The great rebellion against God will grow and grow, characterized by hatred and abuse of what's good and self-interest at the cost of everyone else.

Then the One who will deceive the world will come on the scene, pretending to be the Son of God.

He'll do things that look like amazing miracles and everyone on earth will come under his spell. He'll actively work in opposition to God's good plan in terrible ways like we've never seen before.

Then all the people God created will end up facing this terrible, blazing time of trouble and a lot of people will make the wrong choices and die. But those who continue on, relentless in their belief that God is good and has a good plan, will be rescued because Someone good was called the Punished and took their punishment for them.

The truth of all these predictions will one day appear for everyone to see. Here are some of the signs of this happening:

First, the sky will crack open and peel away. Then, there will be the sound of some great, heavenly trumpet blast. After that, it will be the day of the dead; those who have died will come back to life with new bodies. Excuse me, not all who have died, only those who believed and now belong to the King will be included in this sign of His return.

One day, the world will see all of these things. Yes, and then they'll see the King we serve, walking over the clouds and coming to us.

All this I agree to as Truth.

ACKNOWLEDGMENTS

First and foremost, I want to thank you for reading this little work. We should have coffee and talk sometime.

As it is with so many things in my life, this book would not exist without the hard work and determination of my wife, Robbie. Thank you for being that steady, loving force that propels our family ever forward.

I want to thank my children Jessica, Daniel, Bradley and Janelle, for always encouraging me in my endeavors. You have been an inspiration to me all along the way. How a man like me could ever have such a wonderful family is beyond me and the greatest testimony to God's grace I'll ever know. Your input into this ministry is invaluable to me. Bradley, your editing skills and command of language make me feel simultaneously proud and envious. Jessica, your design skills never cease to bowl me over. Thank you both for the hard work you've invested into this book.

With great gratitude, I want to thank Riley and Lynn, my brother and his wife, for following me out on this crazy limb. We never would have known this fellowship outside of the providence of God and your loving loyalty. Lynn has already finished her journey and I look forward to seeing her there.

All the spiritual vagabonds of Eastgate have my deepest thanks for being who you are and falling in step with this wonderful, wonky parade. You are my family and I don't know where I'd go to church without you.

I'm worried that this whole acknowledgment sounds like I think this book is more than what it is (and believe me, I really don't), but I just want to shout out to those who've shared the leadership of Eastgate with me over the years: Mike and Darby, Lance and Liz, Ron and Kathy, Dan and Patti, Dale and Karen, Matt and Kris, Janelle and Matt, Cole, Luke, Rick and Bonny, Michael and Myra, Kern and Susan, Brian and Kimberly, Dustin and Leah, Larry and Lorry.

What a ride, huh?

Made in the USA
San Bernardino, CA
03 October 2016